The Aftermath
of

Greed

Get Ready
For The Coming

Inflationary

Boom

H. L. Quist

TO RON—
LOOK FORWARD TO
PERSUING OUR GOALS!

7/08

ISBN 978-1-4357-1211-9

www.lulu.com/hlquist

GREED   Blinds us with illusions
                   that we cannot see

FEAR   Immobilizes us so
                   that we cannot act

KNOWLEDGE   Allows us to see illusions,
                   eliminate fear, and
                   realize opportunities

Contents

Acknowledgments & Dedication

Every author enlists assistance from a team of individuals in order to produce a book. Each person has an area of expertise that is essential to complete the end product. I would like to recognize my technical advisor and manuscript typist Catherine Crowley, who has now so capably helped me craft my fourth book. *Greed* has been edited by Mary Hart and my spouse Olivia, whose M.A. in English literature has contributed immensely to the structure of the book. Olivia's thirty year career in real estate has also provided first-hand in-the-trenches experience incorporated herein. To several individuals who must remain anonymous, their forty-plus years of experience in all aspects of the investments business with major Wall Street firms has proven invaluable, as the reader will readily ascertain. Also to Steve Pettit, with whom I've had the pleasure of associating in financial services for many years. And last but not least, many thanks to Burt and Susan Sweetow, the owners of Southwestern School of Real Estate, whose constant support and encouragement gave me the platform and the opportunity to write *Greed.*

This book is dedicated to those in the ranching business, both past and present, who exemplify integrity and honesty in every aspect of their lives. They stand in stark contrast to the unethical and unconscionable behavior of Wall Street, which has exploited America's Middle Class for unreasonable gain and placed the entire economy at risk. Listed here are a few of those families who represent the unwritten "Code of the West" whom I've had the privilege of serving for over forty years:

Fred & Floy Heimann
J. Casper & Owaissa Heimann & Family
Howard & Pauline Robertson & Family
Bobby & Johnann Adee & Family
Dick & Nel Snyder
Manuel & Mary Gonzales
Lavaughn & Otha McDaniel
Bill & Lois Jeffers

In Chapter Eight I quote extensively from James P. Owen's book, "Cowboy Ethics: What Wall St. Can Learn From the Code of the West." I strongly recommend this book.

— H. L. Quist

Preface

The financial markets' history is a trusted teacher, if only it is read and used as a tool to project what lies ahead. As early as 1841 Charles MacKay wrote "Extraordinary Popular Delusions and the Madness of Crowds," which teaches us that human market behavior today is little different from that of hundreds of years ago. But, alas, few were intellectually prepared for the recent predictable turmoil.

Instead, America today wants to be informed in short sound bites. The favorite source for investors and market watchers is CNBC's biased "BUBBLE VISION." Reporters on the widely watched financial news network zealously sing to a choir of advertisers whose objective is to attract and hold the investors' money. Nary a discouraging word is heard until the growl of the Bear drowns out the snorts of the Bull, as we are now witnessing.

"Greed" will hopefully educate many—and maybe anger a few—but too much is at stake to be left unsaid. It's too late for those whose financial life has been destroyed by the Merchants of Debt ... but now armed, or FORE-ARMED, you won't let the bastards do it to you again! And you will be able to seize the opportunities that lie ahead.

Foreword

In the movie "Wall Street," Gordon Gecko (played by Michael Douglas) is a sociopathic Wall Street opportunist who, in one scene speaking to shareholders who are the target of his takeover, declares, "Greed, for lack of a better term, is good for America." Since the release of this film events have occurred that clearly demonstrate, contrary to Gecko's self-serving pronouncement, that greed is *not* good for America. In fact, as the author attempts to illustrate here, greed, or the rapacious desire to accumulate more than one needs, has undermined the basic tenets of our society that has made the American capitalistic system a model and envy of the world.

Clearly, this book is not a tome advocating a radical change in our free enterprise system which has served this nation so well for almost 250 years. The author opines that excess in just about any endeavor will inevitably lead to the denigration and destruction of that endeavor. As a proponent of excess someone once stated, "There is no such thing as having too much sex, too much golf, and too much money." The author disagrees. Excess profits by one class, particularly at the expense or loss of another, is inherently and ethically wrong, and ultimately destructive.

In particular, H. L. Quist traces the origins of "The Greenspan Plan" in the Fall of 2001 to stimulate an economy that was on the cusp of a severe recession, or worse, at that time. The rapid ratcheting down of the discount and the Fed funds rates and the virtual abandonment of reasonable guidelines for underwriting residential real estate loans by the Greenspan-led Federal Reserve created an explosion of real property values in 2003 to the middle of 2006. "Cash Out" residential refinancing became the desired source of stimulus for consumer spending that propelled a lagging economy to illusionary robust growth for the ensuing four years.

By early 2007 the easy-money-driven speculative bubble in U.S. residential real estate had burst. The author, in a "Special Report" dated July 2005, predicted that these events would occur; but commercial banks, mortgage lenders and brokers, real estate marketing firms, and Wall Street Investment Banking firms (to name a few), along with the borrowers, were too absorbed in a borrow-and-spend party never before experienced in the U.S. to pay heed. *Greed* consumed virtually everyone who participated in the money game created by the Fed in 2001. Excess has led to disaster and now threatens the American dream.

Numerous books in retrospect (as always is the case) are now appearing tracing events that led to the greatest crisis in the residential real estate and financial markets since the early 1990s, but H. L. Quist breaks new ground here. One, he directly ties the current boom and bust to Greenspan Fed monetary policy; secondly, he reveals how Wall Street and the mortgage lenders exploited middle class America for exorbitant profits. And finally, the author concludes his book by introducing the possibility of an unexpected inflationary boom that would present unique opportunities.

The author has the ability to dissect the arcane and mysterious machinations of high finance for the average person in a direct, hard hitting, and often humorous style that educates the reader.

— Anon

Introduction

Since so much of our discussion in *Greed* pertains to the "Fed" and the Federal Open Market Committee, it may be helpful to define what the responsibilities of these entities are, who are the individuals who manages them, and how they are appointed to their positions.

The Federal Reserve Act of 1913 enacted by Congress established the Federal Reserve Bank of the U.S. (The "Fed") as its central bank. The Fed is managed by a seven-member Board of Governors. The Chairman (who is now Ben Bernanke—the prior Chairman was Alan Greenspan) and the Vice Chairman are appointed by the President and confirmed by the Senate. The board's responsibility is to form monetary policy. There are twelve Federal Reserve District banks throughout the U.S. Reserve Banks hold the cash reserves of depository institutions and make loans to the commercial banks. They move currency and coin into and out of circulation and collect and process millions of checks each day. They are responsible for supervising and examining the member banks.

The Federal Open Market Committee (FOMC) consists of twelve members: the seven members of the Board of Governors of the Federal Reserve System, the President of the Federal Reserve Bank of New York, and four of the other remaining Reserve Bank presidents who serve on a one-year rotating basis. The purpose of the FOMC is to review economic and financial conditions, determine the appropriate stance on monetary policy, and assess the risks to its long-term goals of price stability and sustainable growth. The FOMC sets both the Discount Rate and the Fed Funds Rate of interest for the member banks.

The Federal Reserve System has a staff of over 2,000 employees and a budget of $300 million. Attending meetings of the FOMC will be their own economists, research assistants, lawyers, and non-voting presidents of the reserve banks.

The obvious questions that seemingly escapes most Americans are:

Q: What do all these men and women have in common?
A. They're all bankers.

Q: What is their primary objective?
A. The profitability and stability of their banks and the banking system.

Q: Why have Citigroup and other major banks lost so much money and created so much instability within the banking system?
A. Citigroup and other major banks have abandoned their core mission and have invested a substantial amount of their capital in high risk assets in search of **Greed**.

Q. What is the potential fallout from this banking crisis?
A. The U.S. banks and Wall Street investment banks have tarnished the country's image and the dollar as a safe haven for investors worldwide. A level of trust has been broken that could inflict irreparable damage on our markets and the U.S. dollar.

.

Chapter One
A History of Boom and Bust Cycles

There have been nine Boom and Bust economic cycles in the U.S. since 1974. What follows is a brief summary of those cycles that prepares the reader for what is to follow. This history has also served as an outline for a real estate continuing education course that I have taught in Scottsdale, Arizona since 1992.

Injected into this thirty-year history is the author's personal experience which mirrors the tumult and the triumph of each period.

1973: The Oil Embargo   Bust

October 17, 1973, should be a day permanently etched in every American's mind. Each day, 85% of all U.S. workers drove to their place of employment. Suddenly, OPEC (the Organization of Petroleum Exporting Countries) announced that they would terminate all export of oil to the U.S. which, even then, was importing 35% of its daily need for petroleum. (It is now over 50%.)

The impact was immediately felt by everyone, including non-employed teenagers who had to curtail their "crusin'." Prices of gasoline increased 400% from about $.30/gallon to $1.20. Fill-ups were limited to 10 gallons per customer. Lines formed for blocks as tempers flared amongst those waiting their turn at the pump. In a short time the fast-moving economic machine in America slowed to a crawl.

The embargo ended on March 18, 1974, lasting six months—and the effects were devastating. The Dow Jones Industrial Average dropped from a high in January 1973 of 1051 to a low of 577 by December, a decline of 45% ... and as market watchers will recall, the stock market went nowhere for several years thereafter.

Is there another oil crisis in the near future? Yes, according to T. Boone Pickins, the legendary oil man who probably knows more about black gold than anyone. Pickins said recently that there is a global depletion rate of oil reserves of 30 billion barrels per year, and the oil industry is nowhere near making new discoveries to replace those reserves. Matt Simmons, the President of Simmons & Co., a Texas consulting firm, is more specific. He says that the Saudis and other OPEC countries are grossly overstating their reserves and that the Saudis' largest field is pumping 50% salt water, a sure sign that the field is experiencing a rapid depletion rate. Peak worldwide oil production reached 74,298,000 BBL in 2005, Simmons figures.

What does this mean to you? Pickins said in 2002 that $3/gallon gasoline was a "certainty." This "liquid tax" will have a dramatic impact on our economy and your pocketbook.

This writer was in the process of moving from Albuquerque, New Mexico, to Phoenix and had already opened an office in Arizona. My bank in Albuquerque (which had financed my expansion) was in deep trouble. Faced with the prospect of closing its doors, the bank called in my (and all) unsecured credit lines. In addition, interest rates rocketed upward, and selling our home became difficult as money became extremely "tight." Added to the oil crisis was the melodrama called Watergate which added another ingredient to the witches' brew of oil, toil and trouble.

Not good times—but more importantly for this book, what was the impact on the real estate market? Our personal experience is probably indicative and instructive.

Our new tri-level 3,500 sq. ft. home, which we had purchased ten years earlier in 1964 for the incredible price of $35,000, sold for $65,000. Considering the backdrop cited above, the sale was remarkable. The purchase of a home in Phoenix was a whole different story.

The vibrant real estate market in Phoenix had crashed. Despite the absence of buyers in the marketplace, however, fixed mortgages remained high in the 12% range. It certainly was a good time to buy—*if* financing could be obtained.

Western Savings & Loan had repossessed 16 townhouses from a builder-developer near 32nd Street and East Camelback, a first-class location. They were holding a fire sale: only $1,000 down and 8%, 30-year, fixed rate financing. We bought the Al Beadle-designed townhouse for only $22/sq. ft.

There was a downside, however, to our successful purchase that I believe represents the market conditions at this point in time. In Western's rush to divest itself of the property on incredible terms, it sold a number of the homes to—let's say euphemistically—unqualified buyers. Today these individuals are referred to as "subprime borrowers," one of the hottest components of today's real estate market that had enormous future consequences. But that comes later.

Many of our new (and interesting) neighbors didn't make their mortgage payments or pay their association dues. There was no money in the treasury to make necessary repairs and maintenance to the complex. My wife and I became (by default) the President and Vice-President of the Association. Our first order of business was to file a lien on our neighbors' properties. We were successful in securing all past-due fees ... not from the homeowners, however. Western Savings & Loan, somewhat complicit in the mess, agreed to reimburse the Association. Ultimately we acquired new and more responsible neighbors, and the project became a delightful place to live. Welcome To The Valley of The Sun 1974.

1977-1980: The Inflationary   Boom

Given the economic turmoil and the bearish market aftermath as a result of the oil embargo, Richard Nixon's disgrace from the Watergate fiasco, and an inoffensive, bland, but capable fill-in President (Gerald Ford), it wasn't a big surprise that an amiable candidate with a decided southern drawl became the next President of the United States. Jimmy Cater assured voters that he would get the economy moving again. He did. Big time!

Carter appointed G. William Miller, a long time friend, as Chairman of the Federal Reserve. They collaborated on a stimulative monetary policy. Long-term fixed mortgage rates (there weren't adjustables at this point in time) declined to the 7 % range. The following three years would produce the largest percentage gain in commercial and residential real estate prices perhaps in U.S. history up to the current time period.

As an example, McCormick Ranch was a 4,200-acre parcel in Scottsdale, Arizona. It was possibly the first land conversion from livestock to residential use in Arizona. It first offered homes for sale in 1971 and 1972 adjacent to two new state-of-the-art, water-oriented golf courses. A typical single family home of 2,000 to 3,000 sq. ft. could be purchased for $60,000 to $100,000. Then, unpredictably, something never experienced in the modern era in the U.S. occurred: prices began rising rapidly.

This phenomenon wasn't confined to residential and commercial real estate. Consumers competed for everything: automobiles, jewelry, art, and just plain "stuff." It seemed that the mantra became "I'd better buy it today, because it will cost more tomorrow." The nation was clearly in a supply-demand inflationary imbalance. Gold, then a barometer of inflation, rose from $100/ounce in 1975 to $850/ounce in 1980.

As residential prices doubled and tripled, homeowners soon discovered newly-created buying power: equity in their homes. By 1978 and 1979, however, mortgage rates had escalated to 10 to 12%. The small first mortgages were 5 to 6%. It was foolish to refinance at twice the cost. What to do? A second mortgage (trust deed) became the source of choice ... then thirds and fourths! What did many homeowners do with the money? They spent it! By 1979 we were witness to a consumer feeding frenzy. Sound familiar?

What is instructive is that the rapidly rising mortgage rates did not deter sales of existing or new homes. I had a meeting with a real estate investor in 1979 who was buying as many properties as he could, and I recall him saying, "What difference does it make if my mortgage is 15% when the land is appreciating 30% per year?" As I looked out of my high-rise office on North Central Avenue in Phoenix, I could see that the sky crane had become the symbolic bird for the city rising from the ashes from the '74 crash.

There is a significant side-bar to this phenomenon that was

occurring right in front of everyone, but few took a step back to analyze its significance. The Consumer Price Index (CPI), which was then a measure of the increases in the prices of all goods and services, had risen from an annual rate of 7% in 1977 to 9% in 1978, 13% in 1979, and 13% in 1980. This index, as complied by the Bureau of Labor Statistics, accurately reflected what was happening in the real world. The index included the increases in the retail prices of home sales. Today it does <u>not</u>. When this government agency currently broadcasts the CPI at 3% for the year, consider it a manufactured number worthless as a guideline for financial planning. The Central Planners in Washington want you to believe that there is no inflation. *The CPI is a cruel hoax, and you're paying the price for their disingenuousness.*

On a personal basis, 1979 offered my wife and me the opportunity to sell our townhouse at a market top. We more than doubled our cost with a sale at $45/sq. ft. I recall sweating out several extensions to our buyer as they had difficulty raising sufficient cash to assume our loan. Because they didn't want buyers to assume their low interest rate loans, lenders were exercising due-on-sale clauses for the first time. Creative financing and "wraps" became necessary to forge a sale.

After selling the townhouse, we purchased an Al Beadle home that he had designed for himself. Despite the fact that we were at a market top, we made the purchase at $66/sq. ft and assumed a 6% mortgage.

As our embassy employees were taken prisoner in Tehran and our beleaguered President had delivered his "malaise" speech, it was obvious to those that were paying attention that the boom that began in 1976 was about to end. The year 1980 marked the end of this cycle.

1980-1981: The S&L Crisis and Stagflation   Bust

Let's assume that you were a shareholder in Western Savings & Loan, Merabank or any other S&L (Thrift) in the U.S. It is 1980. The Thrift has a loan on the books for $100,000 that it made to Mr. and Mrs. Smith in 1970, ten years prior, at 6% (fixed rate). Current mortgage rates in 1980 are now 15%. That loan's value as an asset of the Thrift has to be adjusted downward to compensate for the current market interest rates. Question: What was the present value of the Smith's $100,000 loan in 1980?

    A. $100,000

    B. $ 75,000

    C. $ 40,000

    D. 0

Answer: "C" would be the approximate number.

What is the significance of this exercise? Multiply this number by millions of loans, and the net result is that most of the S&Ls (Thrifts) in the U.S. in 1980 were statutorily bankrupt. If proper accounting rules were applied, they had little or no net worth.

Add to this fact that these thrift institutions borrowed short term and loaned long term. Their cost of funds (COF) had skyrocketed from 7% in 1978 to 11% in 1982. The thrifts were in deep doo-doo.

Another victim of this new-found market dilemma was the hard money lenders. These were the folks who provided some of the fuel for the spending frenzy in the form of second, third and fourth trust deeds. When home values plummeted 20% or more, their loans were underwater (the debt was greater than the value of the home), and the default demon ate their lunch. With no equity in their homes and an inability to make the payments, homeowners 'walked' in droves. Investors who lent the hard money guys their hard-earned cash looking for 12% to 15% returns saw their notes turn to mush. It was a "Lose-Lose" deal.

The situation was dire. It was time for Congress, Wall Street, the Fed, and the "Gipper" (Ronald Reagan) to come to the rescue. The newly elected President signed The Garn-St. Germane Depository Institutions Act of 1982 on October 15, 1982. At a signing in the Rose Garden, the President said:

"This bill is the most important legislation for financial institutions in the last 50 years. It provides a <u>long-term solution</u> for troubled thrift institutions. It's pro-consumer, granting small savers greater access to

loans, a higher return on their savings. And when combined with recent short declines in interest rates, it means help for housing, more jobs, and new growth for the economy. All in all, I think we hit the jackpot."

The Garn-St. Germane Act did hit the jackpot—for shysters and charlatans! For the newly-elected and fiscally naive President, it may have been the source of his famous one-liner:

"Government is not the solution to the problem, government is the problem."

Congress, in passing this legislation, was like a child who wets its bed. The law relieved the immediate pressure, but it created a much larger, long-term problem. Garn-St. Germane provided the key to the bank vault for unscrupulous opportunists like Phoenix' Charles Keating, who was schooled in the use of OPM (other people's money). The thrifts had free rein to diversify their activities. Unburdened by a blatant conflict of interest between their regulatory agency controlled by Congress (FSLIC) and their funding source, the Federal Home Loan Bank Board (FHLBB), the thrifts embarked upon an excessively risky asset diversification plan that would lead to the real estate debacle in 1989-1990. For a brief but insightful understanding of this legislative action and its aftermath go to: www.nysscpa,org/cpajournal/old/14979917.htm and read the report written by Ahmat W. Salam in the January 1994 issue of the CPA Journal.

Salam concludes in his report: "Misguided regulating policies enacted to help the thrift industry in the early 1980s only served to exacerbate the financial troubles of savings and loans later in the decade." Clearly a pattern was being established. A crisis occurs. A temporary solution is provided—but it only sets the stage for a greater tragedy in the future. That future is at hand again in 2007.

A wild ride was also set to begin on Wall Street as the cowboys in suits and ties lassoed residential debt for the first time known as collateralized mortgage obligations (CMOs). For a hilarious and quick read on the "greed, gluttony and outrageous fortunes" and a book that defines this era, read "Liar's Poker" by Michael Lewis. After the read I don't think you'll agree with Gordon Gecko from the movie "Wall Street" that "greed is good for America." A similar voracious appetite of *Greed* devoured our real estate market in 2001 to 2006.

The early 80s was remembered and plagued by a condition dubbed "stagflation." After the wild three-year, double-digit increases in prices the economy slowed dramatically. The worst of both worlds. Higher prices and a slower economy. Real estate entered a dead zone. An absence of buyers in the period of 1980-1982 with high interest rates and declining prices. The stock market began its 18-year bull market in 1982 when conditions appeared to be at their worst. A great opportunity was seized by few.

For years the persuasive mantra in the real estate business has been: *LOCATION, LOCATION, LOCATION*. The implication, presumably, is that if one owned real estate in an excellent location, one would never lose money on their investment. Like many truisms, this well-worn mantra is a myth. Here's just one example:

Under the leadership of an astute and experienced developer, I became a 20% joint venture partner in a project known as Lincoln Resorts. The difficult task was to assemble 30 to 40 acres on Lincoln Drive just two blocks east of Scottsdale Road and the Hilton Hotel. All of the land was zoned residential with approximately 20 existing homes in the area. Many of the homes were in the county and not the City of Scottsdale.

In 1983 Lincoln Resorts began its ambitious project assembling not only the homes in the area specified but approximately 120 acres in the Indian Bend Wash (for a golf course) as well as a number of horse properties fronting on Indian Bend Road. The goal was to acquire all these lands, annex the out-parcels into the City of Scottsdale, and re-zone the entire master-planned project for a five-star hotel, a championship golf course, and approximately 200 single family homes. This mammoth project took four years and a ton of money to bring to the development-ready stage.

1982-1989: The S&L Revival   Boom

By 1985 my investment in the Lincoln Resorts Joint Venture became a full-time occupation. Duties not only included the acquisitions of the properties but working with land planners, neighbors, golf course architects, and governmental agencies including the U.S. Army Corps of Engineers to obtain multi-use zoning for the entire project.

Garn-St. Germane had, in just three years, opened a floodgate of money for projects such as ours all over the land. Office buildings, shopping centers, apartments, and other commercial projects in process were creating a real estate and construction boom—grossly underestimated by those in Washington who provided the keys to the bank. Congress then felt compelled to slow the boom that was in danger of overheating.

The Tax Reform Act of 1986 was passed to "level the playing field" by curbing tax shelters, lowering corporate and individual tax rates, eliminating special treatment for capital gains, and repealing investment tax credits. The good news was that the top marginal tax rate for wealthy individuals was reduced 44%. The bad news was that the Federal deficit ballooned. For real estate syndicators who sold tax shelters, TRA '86 was the death knell. Despite the new law, however, the real estate boom continued unabated.

As indicated above, I was a partner in Lincoln Resorts and Scottsdale Lakes Golf Club. I could write a book about the entire episode but will limit the introspection here to factors that are germane to this piece. In a fast-moving and high stakes casino, however, large projects like ours attracted a whole array of promoters, charlatans, wanna-bees, megastars and plain ol' crooks. Our buyer possessed all those qualities.

Prior to the sale of Lincoln Resorts and the golf course we had secured sources of financing from several banks. One in particular was an $8,000,000 land loan. By 1986 the banks were getting nervous. They feared that the real estate bubble would burst and their portfolio of loans (particularly land loans) would go into default. There are two words that will make a banker shank a golf ball: Depression and Default (Double D).

Upon our obtaining the original land loan, an additional amount was added to the principal to pay interest to the end of the term. When the loan came due and we hadn't secured a sale or refinancing, an additional loan was made to pay interest for the renewed term. This occurred several times. By early 1987, when the bank was not willing to advance additional funds for interest, we entered into "forbearance" agreements which extended the loan and kept it on a "performing status."

The handwriting was on the wall as early as 1987, but ironically banks and thrifts were still aggressively making new loans and doing everything they could to keep the game going. Our sale enabled us to pay off our original land loan. All we had to do was to wait until the end of 1989 and the balloon payment from our buyer—but Congress couldn't wait. The financing frenzy and boom that Congress created in 1982 with the passage of Garn-St. Germane was terminated on August 4, 1989, with the enactment of the Financial Institutions Reform Recovery and Enforcement Act of 1989, known as FIRREA. Banks could no longer make any real estate loans for three years. Congress and the Fed took away the punch bowl that they originally filled with money, and the party was over. It also marked the demise of the thrift industry and the Federal Savings and Loan Insurance Corp. Merabank and Western Savings & Loan closed their doors forever. Who would ever have thunk it?

1990-1992: The Resolution Trust Corp   Bust

The resulting crash was principally experienced in the commercial real estate market. The Resolution Trust Corp (RTC) was formed, and it took possession of all the assets of the failed banks and thrifts. The RTC sold superb properties to "qualified" buyers for discounts ranging from 30% to 60% of the existing debt. It was the greatest write-down of property values and the greatest redistribution of wealth in America since the Great Depression. The use of leverage (borrowed money) to optimize the return on invested capital reversed itself. For those who did not have other resources to pay off leveraged assets, de-leveraging was an extremely painful experience.

What happened to Lincoln Resorts? The Resolution Trust Corp (RTC) took possession of the hotel site and auctioned it off to a well-known local home builder. Their purchase price? Seventy-five percent less than we had <u>sold</u> the land for just three years prior!

What lessons can be learned from this story?

1. All cycles continue until they end.

2. Timing is more important than location.

3. The risk of de-leverage can be greater than the benefits of leverage.

4. Tuition in the real estate business can be very expensive.

In this case, it cost my partner and me millions. But there is a silver lining in every black cloud if you want to weather the next storm. After this experience I took it upon myself to extensively study the markets and discover why boom and bust cycles occur. Are they predicable? How do you know when markets are at a top? At bottom? How can a person prevent loss or profit from them?

The following is an example of one case depicting the Scottsdale, Arizona, residential market at this time. A close friend told me:

"I remember 1990 all too well. I was getting a divorce, and we had to sell our home as part of our settlement. It took forever to sell. The market was dead. We were in a 'dead zone'. It finally sold for 20% less than the listing price."

For some savvy investors who either saw the bust cycle coming or had the resources in waiting, this time period represented one of the best real estate buying opportunities in recent history. Trustee sales were as common as open houses. A large block of single family home sites at Arrowhead Ranch sold for less than $10,000 per lot. Bennett Dorrance, an heir to the Campbell Soup Co. fortune and an Arizona resident, entered the real estate development business in a major way. He quipped at the time, "I'll either make a fortune or go belly-up." Obviously, his timing couldn't have been better. As the country found itself between Iraq and a hard place in the Persian Gulf, the markets were also taking a dramatic twist elsewhere.

During the 80s boom the Japanese were buying trophy real estate all over the world and particularly in the U.S. They paid almost one billion dollars for Pebble Beach, bought the Rockefeller Center in New York City, and invested $100 million in the largest white elephant in Arizona known as The Galleria in Scottsdale. They willingly paid top market price for properties because they were "long-term investors." Within a few years the Japanese were forced to sell or abandon most all of their holdings in the U.S. Location was meaningless.

In December 1989 the Japanese stock market topped out just a shade under 40,000. Reacting, in part, to the loss of consumer buying power for its exports, the Nikkei began a plunge that would result in a 70% loss in a couple of years. Several years later the commercial and residential real estate market began a similar dive that would take it down by an equal amount. Remarkably, 14 years later both markets remained off over 50% from their January 1990 highs. Japan was in a severe recession. For those who scoff at the idea that a protracted contraction cannot reoccur in America, check out the Japanese experience.

1992-1999: The Feel Good Era   Boom

To the reader the correlation of politics to boom and bust cycles should now be quite apparent. On election day 1991 George Bush (the elder) was faced with an economy that was in the toilet at the bottom of the bust cycle elucidated above. Mr. Bush was also credited with reneging on his no-tax increase ("read my lips") promise. As Bill Clinton exploited, "It's the economy, stupid." It was, with a then record annual federal budget deficit of $280 billion. His son G.W., 15 years later, would relish such a low number.

True to form, however, in the world of politics, the Clinton Congress immediately passed the Tax Reform Act of 1993. Americans suffered the largest tax increase in history which became one of the cornerstones of the "Feel Good Era" that was to unfold over the next eight years.

In the late 90s I wrote a story about a golfer and a fictional president entitled <u>SECRETS, A Novel Of Golf & Politics</u>. My fictitious president had an uncanny resemblance to Bill Clinton. On page 148 I wrote:

"When J.P. was elected, he was determined that he would not suffer the same fate as President Carter. Fourteen percent inflation and a 21 percent prime rate made Carter a one-term President. He lost control of the economy. Before he took office, J.P. called a meeting of economists, bankers, Wall Street types, the Fed Chairman and his prospective cabinet and forged his "Dream Team." J.P. said if they all worked together as a 'Team,' they and their clients could all get rich. In order for everything to come together and to keep him in office for eight years, there couldn't be any inflation. J.P. made sure that there wouldn't be. By 'cooking the books,' the 'Team' created a perception that there wasn't any inflation and perception became reality."

The second cornerstone of Clinton's fiscal policy was to find jobs for ten million Americans in his first term. He needed the cooperation of the Federal Reserve and the Treasury Department in order to avoid inflation and higher interest rates. In 1995 he called in a Wall Street maven by the name of Robert Rubin who guaranteed the optimum fiscal conditions to perpetuate the "Feel Good Era" and a second term for the President. Rubin as Secretary of the U.S. Treasury quickly announced that "a strong dollar was in the best interest of America."

Rubin's plan focused on two key results:

1. Foreign capital would pour into U.S. assets including treasuries, real estate, and securities causing asset prices to rise and providing foreign investors leverage on their own currency; and

2. Imported products would be cheaper, thus assuring that consumer prices would remain flat or moderate, there would be "no inflation," and

interest rates would remain low.

Few economists, market analysts, or political pundits realized then that there would be a negative and devastating impact from the "strong dollar policy" on U.S. manufacturing jobs. What was a trickle of outsourcing in 1995 became a flood early in the 21st Century. Rubin takes kudos for the economy's dividends but takes no blame for the devastation of blue-collar jobs.

I was teaching a real estate continuing education class in 1992 when I told the students that a reason for my optimism was that FIRREA had expired. Banks now could make real estate loans. It was time for developers, builders, real estate agents, speculators and everyone involved in the business to position themselves for the boom years ahead, but it appeared that only a few people possessed the knowledge, the vision, and the capital to get a jump on their competition. It's almost axiomatic:

1. When markets are at the bottom of a bust cycle no one thinks they'll ever get better.

2. When markets are at the top of a boom cycle no one thinks that they'll ever end.

There was other first-hand evidence to support my position. Another joint venture in which I was a 20% partner had a strategically located and zoned parcel in the heart of Scottsdale. For three years there was not a single inquiry to buy the property at **any** price. Suddenly in January 1993, as FIRREA expired, numerous offers came in. Each one was better than the prior.

During the crash many builders folded their tents and went out of business. Most of those left standing had little or no inventory. Raw land was in demand. I saw a great opportunity to improve the land and sell lots to builders in order to maximize our investment. My partner, drained emotionally and financially from the bust, wanted out ... and we made a cash sale at a loss. The project built on this site was a great success. Timing again was key.

This is not to imply that the period from 1993 to 1999 was an irrational boom real estate market ... it was not. It was orderly and liquid.

Most residential sales were negotiated below listed price, and appreciation was within long-term norms at 3% to 5% increases per year. What was a buyer's market in the early 90s was soon to again become a seller's environment.

As the November 1999 election approached, the second quarter drop in the Gross Domestic Product (GDP) demonstrated that the economy was cooling. Events were about to occur that would end the "Feel Good Era" and rain on the inaugural parade of George Bush II.

2000-2001: The .com Bubble and 9-11   Bust

Given my partner's desire to exit the development business in Scottsdale in 1993, I made the decision to return to the financial services business in which I was successfully involved for the prior 23 years.

It was March 2000. I was having lunch with a new client at the Stonecreek Golf Club. CNBC and Market Watch were on the TV screen precariously poised over our heads. The Dow Jones Industrial Average was down 500 points. The NASDAQ plunged 300 points.

"Wow! That's quite a correction," my new client exclaimed.

"This is not a correction, Susan. This is the beginning of the bear market," I replied. And so it was. The bell I was certain would ring had just rung that day, but few heard it.

The Federal Reserve, fearful of a Y2K run on the banks, had injected $60 billion into the banking system in the last quarter of 1999 which manifested itself in a bull market "blow off" in March and April 2000. Every day, seemingly everyone everywhere was justifying to themselves and anyone who would listen that this was only a correction. "It is different this time," they reasoned. "We're in a new technological era," they said. "All the old rules didn't apply anymore," they argued. Who were "they?" Those whose vision was impaired. I called the condition "fecalopia."

Again, I would like to refer to SECRETS, a Novel of Golf and Politics which was released two months prior to the bursting of the .com bubble. My hero Robbie e-mails his friend Tom in Phoenix:

"The Communists and the Socialists call 'cooking the books' Central Planning. No one in Russia, except the ruling elite, knew the country was broke until the wall came down. But you can only lie for so long. Historically, all manipulated markets end badly. This bubble is going to implode causing a world-wide panic..."

After a meeting with a Wall Street firm, Robbie again e-mails Tom:

"Met with the big dogs on Wall Street. I had to ask some provocative questions so I could read the sub text. Some of them actually have the same concerns as I do, but their mantra has to be that the market is going higher. They're trying to convince themselves that the derivatives are not a problem since they're such a big player in that market. The hedge funds and banks have created a huge inverted pyramid that is leveraged 200 to 300 to one. It won't take much to topple the pyramid. Just like dominoes. There are ten to fourteen thousand tons of gold sold short as part of the strategy to convince everyone there is not inflation but if the price goes up, the pyramid crumbles and the banks that have loaned billions to the hedge funds, could go bell-up. The 'Dream Team' with their manipulation, has put all America at risk."

When the dust cleared from the crash, the NASDAQ lost over 70% of its value. The Dow and the S&P-500 lost almost 50% from their record tops. Analysts estimate that approximately $4 to $6 *trillion* in perceived equity vanished from March 2000 to October 2002. To me, this crash was a no-brainer event, and my clients at that time avoided significant loss and grief. Most advisers now say they saw the crash coming. Few said it in writing.

When the Dow plunged 50% in just three days in October 1987, the real estate market bust followed two years later. Would history repeat itself? We never got a chance to find out. September 11, 2001, was a second day in our lifetimes that would go down in infamy.

Chapter Two
The Greenspan Plan
(A Flawed Strategy)

A year following the tragedy of September 11, 2001, shock, fear, and anger permeated the country. Not an ideal environment to ignite confidence to create a robust economy. The nation was on the verge of a recession or worse, and a depression loomed as a distinct possibility. Here are a few excerpts from the Federal Reserve Board's Open Market Committee Meeting (FOMC) on September 24, 2002.

"At its meeting on August 13, 2002, the Committee retained a directive that called for maintaining conditions in reserve markets consistent with keeping the intended level of the Federal funds rate at 1-3/4 percent, but it shifted from a statement of neutral balance of risks to one that was tilted toward economic weakness in the foreseeable future..."

Despite the gloomy pall that had been cast over our land by these two history making events (the stock market crash and 9/11) there emerged a beacon of light that gave the Fed a source to buttress the economy against the dreaded "Double D"—Depression and Default.

The consumer had discovered an ATM at their doorstep. Again, from the same FOMC Meeting:

"The value of homes had continued to rise in most areas, and unusually low interest rates were inducing people to refinance mortgages and in the process to extract and spend some of the embedded gains. Increasing home equity values probably were also providing some counterweight to the impact of consumer spending of the negative wealth effects associated with the declines in stock prices since the spring of 2000..."

Economists maintain that consumer spending is 66% of the entire Nation's Gross Domestic Product (GDP). Normally, folks (as average Americans, given the backdrop of uncertainty spawned by these two nasty events) would elect to be conservative in their spending habits—particularly discretionary spending—and would be motivated to add to their rainy day fund. That type of conventional wisdom was not acceptable in this 21st Century "New Economy." Certainly not acceptable to a banking industry whose propellant for growth was the creation of debt. The "cash out" refinance era was born in the dark days of 2002. President Bush's advice? "Go shopping."

Perhaps there was a reverse psychological hook that made folks feel better when they satisfied their urge to splurge rather than save. Who knows? One thing is certain: the "New Economy" redefined the term liquidity. In the olden days, liquidity used to be cash or assets that could easily be converted to cash. What was about to occur was the creation of an illusion that credit availability was the same as cash, and it could be obtained by a stroke of a pen.

You will recall the TV ads that enticed the viewer to be "DEBT FREE." Prior to this period, a plethora of plastic had been the credit availability of choice. "Rolling Over" from one card to another was creating maxed-out conditions and an angst in the banking community. The REFI phenomenon made its way into our lexicon and consciousness by the repetitive and pervasive inference that cash-out refinancing our home was our ticket to a debt-free existence. The bankers (and their alter-ego, The Fed) were ecstatic! Americans would enthusiastically jump at the chance to dig themselves into a deeper hole of debt to get the bankers out of the one *they* were already in.

You may recall the hit TV program called "The Mod Squad" which enjoyed enormous success from 1968 to 1973, principally due to its timing in an era of student unrest and anti-war sentiment. The Squad was made up of three young, troubled kids who had dropped out of conservative society and became "flower children." They reversed their direction to become a special youth police squad to infiltrate the counter culture. They were the "fuzz" in bell bottoms. They were the good guys.

What does the "Mod Squad" have to do with **Greed**?

It's admittedly a stretch, but the turn of the century is marked by a new MOD SQUAD—The Merchants of Debt (MOD). In a 180° role reversal a number of these bankers, investment bankers, mortgage companies, and mortgage brokers whose original goal may have been to meet a worthy need became predatory lenders in search of **Greed**. They're the new MOD SQUAD—but they're the *bad guys*. They're the focus of this book and hereafter are simply identified as MOD.

Congress, ever cognizant of who butters their bread, added legislation that also hastened the borrow-and-spend campaign that would ply its constituents. It passed The American Down Payment Dream Act, which was a Federal handout to first-time home buyers of up to $10,000 available to anyone with an income 20% less than the median income in their locality. A gift that was supplied by taxpayers. In the San Francisco Bay area, a family of four with an income up to $113,000 qualified for this freebie.

Congress also passed a 100% Tax Credit for consumers as an incentive to buy a 5,000 pound gas-guzzling Hummer or SUV at a time when fuel conservation would have been somewhat more prudent. The automobile industry, perhaps wary that the consumer was getting wise to the purported interest-free loans, got its wish and moved the heavy inventory despite the $3.00/gallon gasoline. It wasn't the first time, nor the last, that Congressional wisdom conflicted with sound economic strategy.

In the whole scheme of things these incentives to borrow and spend couldn't hold a candle to what creative products the mortgage bankers, cognizant of the goals of the President and the Greenspan Plan, could conjure up. The Adjustable Rate Mortgage (ARM) was perhaps the primary precursor of a wealth of products that would follow. Shortly after the September 2002 FOMC meeting the Discount Rate and the Fed Funds rates were reduced to one percent. A 40-year low enabled the initial ARMs to be advertised below two percent. Many readers will recall that it was the

Chairman himself, the usually obscure Alan Greenspan, who publicly advised in clear and concise terms that homeowners refinance their homes utilizing the ARM—a message that should have carried a 'FORE-warning disclaimer.'

In itself there's nothing indecent or immoral in an ARM, but the consumer apparently ignored the key word—*adjustable*. The Chairman's enthusiastically-received recommendation couldn't have come at a worse time. With the Fed Funds and the Discount Rate at 40-year lows of one percent and Treasury Notes on a flat yield curve with similar yields, rates had only one way to go: UP ... unless, of course, the Chairman's crystal ball or his soothsayers lacked the conviction that the economy would rebound from the doldrums. In the past, conservative underwriting guidelines required the borrower to make at least a 10% down payment, had demonstrated that the borrower was historically fiscally responsible, and the debt service was approximately 25% of the borrower's income. Given the parameters, the mortgagor (that's you) would have been in reasonably good position to absorb a 20% or 30% increase in the monthly mortgage payment. The ARM alone wasn't the deal killer. The mortgage lending industry went from creative to absurd, and the home became an ATM and a speculator's dream. Wall Street also got the scent of money and would soon become the enabler that made it all so easy.

An interest-only loan is precisely what the term implies. There will be no principal reduction in the loan until the term of the loan ends. The interest (fixed or variable) was due at the end of the term. Applying this product to residential real estate for a longer term (10 years) was a new concept. Obscured by the marketplace and even by the MOD was the birth of a new philosophy promulgated by the bankers in the New Economy. Residential real estate loans need no longer be amortized. This would not provide the homeowner with an increase in equity each month and hopefully at some point in time (in retirement) a debt-free residence, but that was now irrelevant.

Bankers enthusiastically embraced the new concept that residential loans would be repaid from refinancing and not from income. In the new world of finance the MOD created loans to roll over and not be retired in conventional terms. Absolute genius! Heck, no one lives in one place very long anyways, huh?

This concept was based upon the premise that:

1. Real property values would continue to appreciate or, at a minimum, remain the same as when the loan was originated.

2. The residential market would remain liquid, and the buyer/borrower would have little trouble selling the property or refinancing elsewhere.

This premise, like those to follow, were flawed. Why should we be surprised? But millions are.

After the meltdown in the real estate market in 1990 (The Resolution Trust Period), bankers focused on a niche market that had gone undiscovered. Not only did homeowners lose their homes during this period, but many lost their cars. Under FIRREA, banks were prohibited from making real estate loans, but there was a fertile field of prospective car buyers who had lousy credit. They were happy to pay 20% to 30% interest only to have "wheels." They were also diligent in making their payments, as credit was scarce as hen's teeth. The banks and the auto dealers were delirious. What they didn't realize, of course, was that they not only discovered a niche market for auto loans but also opened the door to subprime credit in the real estate sector 12 years later.

Auto loans reached a new pinnacle in our New Economy also. You've seen the ads on TV and heard them on the radio:

"No credit, bad credit and no matter what you owe on your present car, we'll get you into a new car today."

Bankers are an amazing bunch to watch. Their herd mentality is to be the first at number two. They observe a sibling pioneer in a new market, and if that bank survives intact without arrows in its back the brothers rush in to share in the spoils. Subprime auto loans, like real estate soon to follow, were case in point.

Originally, the bankers filled a need and performed a service to a segment of society that had a major deterrent to finding work or enjoying some of the joys of life. What has been developed in the New Economy is all financing has been taken to excess. Car lots are loaded with "repos." How many more can the banking industry absorb? Does anyone care? Has the write down of bad loans become irrelevant? Stay tuned.

"Alt A Loans" are a credit class between Prime and Subprime—those with "blemishes" on their credit history. Subprime would be those with a proven record of not fulfilling their commitments on time. Meeting the needs of this market apparently didn't meet the needs of a lower special class of borrowers—those who couldn't or wouldn't disclose any information on themselves to a lender. Thus, the "no-doc" loan was created for these individuals who could be best described as "phantoms."

No Doc (document) loans were last utilized by hard money lenders in the late 1980s who specialized in second and third trust deeds. Despite the fact that most of these lenders crashed and burned when the real estate bubble burst in 1990, mass dementia prevented the odious experience refreshing the MOD senses in 2002.

One of the best instances of a "No Doc" loan was not one but three loans made to a convicted felon who just happened to be residing in a state penitentiary when the loans were made. The revelation came to the lender, while preparing to make a fourth loan, who discovered that his Subprime borrower had not made a payment on the first loan. No checking account, perhaps?

So, in a brief period of time from mid-2002 to 2003, armed with every device and product to fulfill the objectives of the Greenspan Plan, the MOD set in motion the greatest increase in real property values the nation had ever experienced. The cash-out refinance of residential real estate and the subsequent consumer buying binge far exceeded the Fed's, the FOMC's, and economists' objectives and estimates. Happy days were here again—or so everyone believed.

In addition to the above-cited Chairman Alan Greenspan, the Fed had on its Board of Governors a man by the name of Ben Bernanke, whose flippant comments in the fall of 2002 somehow failed to disqualify him as the next Federal Reserve Board Chairman. The media gave the to-be-Chairman the moniker "Helicopter Ben" when he spoke to the National Economics Club in Washington, D.C. on November 2, 2002, and envisioned dropping dollars from a helicopter in order to avoid a deflationary recession.

In another speech the future Chairman was quoted as saying "The U.S. Government has a new technology called "The Printing Press" that allows it to produce as many dollars it wishes at essentially no cost."

He regrets making those comments out of context.

To me, as an investor trying to assess risk and opportunity, it meant one thing. Get 100% invested. The Fed was going balls-to-the-wall to inflate all assets. Sure enough, that's exactly what happened. We had the bowl, the Fed had the punch, and the party was on!

Chapter Three
The New Economy
(An Illusion)

Once upon a time, not long ago in a land nearby, there reigned an emperor who possessed great financial power, and everyone in his kingdom and throughout the entire world listened to every word he ever said. The emperor was fascinated by clothes and believed that his appearance as well as his wisdom was a sign of his nation's wealth. One day, two charlatans came to the emperor and told him that they had the most luxurious material ever known to man and they would tailor a suit for the emperor that would demonstrate and exude the riches of the land. This special material, they assured the emperor, had a unique quality. It would be invisible to anyone who was either too stupid or unfit for his position in the kingdom.

Concerned whether or not he himself would be able to see the special clothes, the emperor sent several members of his trusted board of directors to view the material. None of them, of course, would admit that they couldn't see the cloth, so they praised it highly. All of the emperor's subjects soon heard about the special cloth and certainly wanted to know how stupid their fellow countrymen were.

Finally a most important day arrived and the emperor, not wanting to admit that he was stupid and unfit to rule the land, delivered a speech in front of his minions declaring that the nation was rich and everyone was doing well.

All the people were happy to hear that they were experiencing good fortune and they praised the magnificent clothes he was wearing, reluctant to admit that they could not see them, until a small child yelled out:

"The emperor has no clothes!"

Everyone gasped. The emperor, embarrassed by the illusion he had created, retired and wrote a book.

So, what's to be learned from this adaptation of "The Emperor's New Clothes" fable by Hans Christian Anderson?

Alan Greenspan, alias the emperor, in his eighteen-year reign as Chairman of the Federal Reserve Board has, in the opinion of many (who didn't want to appear stupid), reigned over and in fact created a robust economy. Critics, like little boys with doctorate degrees, and even former Fed members are taking a fresh view. The New Economy of Greenspan's creation is an illusion, they say. Worse, the economy may be headed for a colossal collapse. By golly, maybe then the emperor truly *didn't* have any clothes!

If anyone had made this assertion at the end of 2005, their claim would have been met with derision and disdain. After all, residential property values in some areas of the country had seen appreciation rates of 20 to 30% per year for the past three years. Our neighbors' home in Phoenix sold for $1,200,000 in 2006. Since our home has the same square footage and is registered in the Modern Museum of Art (Google H. L. Quist), that would have indicated that our home had at least doubled in value in those three years. Nice thought, but my wife Olivia and I never bought into the market mania of the New Economy. Olivia is a realtor with 30 years experience and a healthy market perspective. Olivia has also served as Chairman of the Ethics Committee for the Scottsdale Board of Realtors. Those numbers were a temporary illusion. We never tapped into our equity and, blessed with the fact that my lovely spouse hates to shop, we never were influenced by the deliberate creation of the "wealth effect" that pushed the consumers' buttons.

How about the stock market? The Dow Jones Industrial Average (DJIA) closed the year at 8,304 on December 31, 2002. By the end of 2006 the index finished at 12,403 ... an increase of 4,099 points or a return of 49% over the three-year period. You could probably have thrown darts at a list of the big board stocks and made a decent return. And what about commodities? A boom was missed by the average investor as base metals such as copper, zinc, nickel, and other metals doubled and tripled. Precious metals skyrocketed. Gold rose from $349/oz. at December 31, 2002, to $638/oz. at December 31, 2006. Oil appreciated from $32.72/barrel to $61.05/barrel.

So, given the historic appreciation of all these asset classes, how could anyone make a claim that this appreciation was an illusion? Without being somewhat pedantic, a little background is necessary.

Most Americans know very little about the money they carry in their purses and wallets, but it's time you made a discovery. The "force" is against you, however. You've seen the TV ad promoting VISA where everyone is zipping through a deli lunch line flashing their cards in front of a digital reader when an Old Economy dork pulls out cash and throws a monkey wrench into the whole system. Bankers want a cashless society. Spend more, faster, and pay later—with interest.

Way back in the olden days of 1913 and the passage of the Federal Reserve Act, the federal government ceded the power over our money (specifically granted to it by the U.S. Constitution) to private interests. The first thing you need to know is that the Fed is **not** a government agency. The Constitution gave only Congress the power to coin money and to regulate its value—but a well-orchestrated *coup d'etat*, on the last day before Congressional Christmas recess in 1913, forever changed our money system to private interests. The Fed Chairman is not a government servant. He serves at the discretion of the President and defers to the will of the money center banks and the Wall Street power brokers, as you will soon discover. Armed with this knowledge you will understand why we have arrived at such a perilous state in the New Economy. And the paper money in your pocket is becoming worth less and less—i.e., worthless.

If you would like a thorough and intriguing in-depth analysis of the Fed, I would highly recommend "The Creature from Jeckyl Island" by G. Edward Griffin. It's a non-fiction mystery story.

A more specific definition of the New Economy would be helpful at this juncture.

Remember, this isn't about parties and politics or voodoo economics—and it's not as difficult to understand as you may think. We're talking about your pocket book, your financial security, your retirement, and, in fact, your future. **Pay attention!** As if I didn't have to ask.

You've probably heard the expression 'the U.S. dollar is declining in value.' What does that mean? More importantly, what does that mean *to you*? Again, a little history will be helpful.

As Bill Clinton focused upon his re-election in 1994, he was concerned that the economic stimulus plans put in place in the previous three years, plus the impact of NAFTA (The North American Free Trade Agreement), might overheat the economy (re-read the <u>Feel Good Era</u>). Lloyd Bentsen, the Secretary of the U.S. Treasury, had served in the position for the first three years of Clinton's term and was a moxy, masterful politician— but, unfortunately, not a heavyweight in the complicated and duplicitous game of international finance. Clinton, wanting to assure his re-election, needed to call in the "A" Team. He called upon the top man at the most powerful investment banking firm in the world to develop a new strategy. Enter one Robert Rubin, then Chairman of Goldman Sachs (now known in some circles as Goldman-Sucks, an intended double-entendre). Ironically, after George Bush II brought in two treasury secretaries who also failed to serve their President as he intended, he too turned to Goldman Sachs to manage his fiscal policy. More on that later.

As stated earlier, Rubin quickly announced: "...a strong dollar was in the best interest of America."

Rubin's plan focused on two key issues:

- Attract foreign capital that would acquire U.S. assets including treasuries (to pay the Nation's bills), real estate, and securities causing asset prices to rise and providing foreign investors leverage on their own currency, and
- Lower the cost of imported products that would be cheaper, thus assuring that U.S. consumer prices would remain flat or moderate. The net result there would be no "visible" inflation, and interest rates would remain low.

I won't repeat what was said earlier other than to emphasize that what was a trickle of jobs lost offshore prior to 1994 became a flood from then to the current date. And, equally important, the trade deficit ballooned each year, reaching nearly *one trillion dollars* in 2006 from the cheap imports of toys, clothing, tech services, and just about everything we consume from fish to pharmaceuticals. Our manufacturers simply couldn't compete because of the strong dollar policy. Bottom line—it was a short-term fix principally motivated for political reasons that proved to be devastating to blue-collar America. The chief beneficiary was, of course, The People's Republic of China, whose new capitalistic-styled economy blossomed as their orders and trade surplus soared.

The dynamics of the dollar reversed beginning in late 2001 and 2002. The Euro was introduced January 1, 1999, which was a single currency for the European Union's original 13 countries (now 27). In 2000 the U.S. dollar would buy about .94 Euros. Today it buys about .69 Euros, a drop in value of the dollar of over 40%. If you went to Europe recently you probably suffered sticker shock. You may have paid $12 or more for a Big Mac. I spent several weeks in Sweden in 2002. One dollar bought 10 Kroner then. Now, it will only buy six.

Okay, let's get down to the nitty-gritty. How does the declining dollar impact you?

Tens of millions of Americans have lost jobs to outsourcing. Maybe you were one of those unfortunate statistics. The Bureau of Labor (BOL) reports that unemployment is running at approximately 4.6%, which historically is extremely low. What that highly questionable number does not tell you is what the loss of earnings has been from one occupation to another since that person is still employed (or employed part-time). You may have been a skilled auto worker or craftsman previously making $40 to $60/hour but have had to accept a job making a little as $10 to $20/ hour. Also, like every other government reporting agency, the BOL's full employment numbers are skewed to present a favorable picture. Those who have been unemployed for a period of six months no longer appear as unemployed. In the past year hundreds of thousands of residential construction workers, retail employees supporting home construction companies like Home Depot or Lowes, employees at mortgage companies and banks, appraisers and real estate agents, and a whole list of white-collar workers have been laid off with the collapse of the residential real estate market. How can the U.S. and BOLS report full employment when so many are losing their jobs? And the 'dirty li'l secret' in America today is that the average earnings of men is $35,000/year. Their fathers made $40,000 in the 1970s, when you could buy a Chevy or Ford sedan for about $4,000.

A falling dollar is another word to describe inflation. Inflation is the loss of purchasing power. Here again the Bureau of Labor Statistics (BOLS) issues monthly the Consumer Price Index, which is purported to be a fairly representative list of all the items we consume. Please refer to Chapter One for the period 1977-1980 when the BOLS reported the true unadjusted inflation rate for the last time—a 13% year-over-year increase in the cost of goods and services for three years from 1978 to 1980.

One single issue more than any other prompted the government to begin to "cook the books" in 1980. If you were over age 65 in 1980 and receiving $1,000/ month in Social Security retirement benefits at the end of the government fiscal year ending September 30, 1979, your check for the following year would have been increased to $1,130/ month—a 13% increase. Similar increases had been occurring for the prior three years. Policy wonks in Washington alerted Congress that if these increases continued much longer the Social Security Trust Fund would go bankrupt. So, here is what the Central Planners did to reduce the future payments.

During the late 1970s, home prices had appreciated significantly, as pointed out earlier. Those increases were recorded properly as part of the CPI. In 1981 the sale prices of homes were excluded from the index, and in their place was substituted an index referred to as Homeowners Equivalent Rent, or HER. Jokingly, the BOLS wanted to reduce HER spending.

The HER simply computes the change in the rents charged on single family residences across the country which (this will surprise no one), are minuscule. Given the explosion in home prices over the past four years (2003-2007), how has this impacted the average American?

Remember, virtually all entitlement programs are indexed to the CPI as well as some wages, rents on commercial buildings, and the like. While home prices were going through the roof, incomes were flat or modestly higher. When folks were applying for a home loan, their combined income had to be stretched (or in many cases altered) to qualify for an ARM. There's an obvious disconnect between wages and property values caused by the creation of cheap, easy credit while the true CPI is probably two or three times greater than the 2% reported by BOLS every year.

Sandra Ward, in a Barron's feature article "Investing in a Shaky World," interviewed Rudolph-Riad Younes, the Co-Manager of Julius Baer International Equity Fund. He said:

"Core inflation should also include house prices and other asset prices, rather than just rental equivalents, as is done now. Again, that would change the inflation picture dramatically. If you consider headline inflation and include asset prices, the true inflation number would be between 7% and 10%." [1]

If, as Younes says, inflation rates are four times greater than the number stated by BOLS, you can begin to appreciate the severe problem faced by middle-class America. A very large number of these folks are borrowing to cover their true cost of living, while Wall Street and the elite class of investors thrive on the phony data.

People see and feel the pain when they fill their gas tank. BOLS removes fuel and food prices from the "core" of the index to further create the illusion that there is no inflation. In the past year, eggs are up 38%, milk 30%, lettuce 17%, cheese 12%, whole wheat bread 12%, etc. In addition, health care and prescription drugs have increased over 10 to 15% per year, plus a host of other products and services far exceeding that 2% number. Now you know why you are being squeezed every month.

So when you hear the talking heads on CNBC and other financial shows constantly crowing that inflation is under control, it is no wonder that America is rapidly losing faith in its leadership. They're lying to us for their own self-serving agenda, which we'll soon discuss. Inflation rates are currently rising in South America, and they could see a repeat of the hyper-inflation rates over 1,000% in the 1980s. The U.S. could also be on the precipice of a sudden surge in inflation similar to the late 1970s (Chapter Ten).

Perhaps the biggest threat to a declining dollar is foreign sales of U.S. assets, particularly our Treasury Bonds. The U.S. Treasury is borrowing about $2 billion dollars *per day* to keep the ship of state afloat. Foreign governments such as China stand to lose money three ways on their investment in U.S. assets. First, as each one of us Americans loses purchasing power we're going to buy less from China. Second, with the recent disclosure of all the contaminants in China's products, U.S. citizens are mad as hell and are seeking alternative sources. Third, as our dollar declines, the value of the assets they're holding also declines. Since the U.S. is China's number one customer, at some point they're going to diversify out of the dollar. In early November 2007 Xu Jian, an official at China's Central Bank, announced, "We will favor stronger currencies over weaker ones." Let's face it. China has Uncle Sam by the short hairs (on his chinny chin-chin), and they can yank it at any time. Credit all those globalists, bankers, and politicians who made us so vulnerable.

Almost 25 years ago the bankers and the politicians in Hong Kong and the U.S. decided to peg the Hong Kong dollar to the U.S. dollar (USD). The two currencies then moved in tandem. The massive inflows of investment capital into China and its booming economy, coupled with the sharp decline of the USD, has brought considerable pressure on the Hong Kong Monetary Authority (HKMA) to modify or even sever the peg with the USD. The prospect for a currency crisis is omni-present with inflation beginning to skyrocket in China, which could trigger a much-overdue correction in the Asian stock markets.

Charles Schurmer, Congressman from New York, wants to slap a 27% tariff on all Chinese goods imported by the U.S. Our new Secretary of the Treasury, Henry Paulson, another wizard from Goldman Sachs, is pressuring China to revalue its currency (the Yuan) upward. China probably won't respond until after the Olympics in the summer of 2008 ... but then: watch out! Major changes could occur, including an invasion of Taiwan by China. None of them will be positive for the U.S. and our dollar.

And what about the "Loonie?" The Canadian dollar coin is so named because it has a loon on its back. As a youngster of 13 I had the good fortune to spend a week in Canada. As the sun completed its descent on Lake Louise, I heard the plaintive and almost humanly haunting cry of the loon. As the U.S. dollar has imploded against the Loonie, it now enjoys an 8% premium to the USD and has gained 16% against the USD in 3 months. The cry is from our northern cousins who have lost more than 40% on their U.S. dollar investments. Thomas G. Donlan, the Editorial Page Editor of Barron's, isn't as polite as your author. I believe that he summarizes the situation best when he says:

"Why is Canada's Loonie up and the greenback down? Doesn't the U.S. have a "strong dollar policy?" Actually it has liars in high office..."

It always seems that there's a pop culture seminal event that highlights a major trend or quite possibly marks the end of a trend or a bottom of a cycle. One of the world's top fashion models, Brazilian Gisele Bundchen (Tom Brady's squeeze), reportedly has requested that her $33 million dollar contract be paid in euros and not dollars. You wouldn't expect the world's number one fashionista to purchase the latest French couture in dollars! How *gauche*! As for a signal that a bottom of a cycle had been reached, some pundits surmised that the only bottom of notice was that of Gisele.

The Arab petroleum producers are already making a move, and some have requested payment for their oil in euros, not dollars. Kuwait, a friendly nation to the U.S., is liquidating its portfolio of U.S. Treasury Bonds along with Sweden. Unfriendly nations such as Venezuela have sold their Bonds. Foreign banks are concerned that the U.S. fiscal and monetary policy is out of balance and in disarray. And it is.

So what happens when and if this occurs? A sudden rise in interest rates will occur. Given a time when Wall Street, mortgage bankers, hedge funds, and consumers are expecting declining rates, an unexpected rise would be a knockout punch to the jaw of Uncle Sam and would increase the probability of a recession. Details to follow—along with smelling salts.

Inflation is a monetary phenomena. As Bernanke suggested, the government (more correctly, the Fed) has at its disposal the printing press. It simply creates money out of thin air at little or no cost and then charges its member banks interest to borrow it. Today, it's much easier for the Fed. It creates money through a click of a mouse and cancels debt by hitting a delete button.

The Fed recently made the arbitrary decision to not publish certain money supply numbers (M3), knowing full well the double-digit increases would up the Fed watchers' queeze factor. Critical data will become less transparent in the future despite Mr. Bernake's announcement to the contrary.

Money, in a sense, is a commodity. It's like peanuts. If farmers grow too many peanuts and flood the market, the prices they receive for their crops will be less. Jimmy Carter, the nation's most recognizable peanut farmer, discovered this fact when he over-stimulated the economy as elucidated earlier. The Fed has flooded not only our economy but also the world with trillions of fiat (paper) U.S. dollars that have no underlying value other than the U.S. Treasury's promise to pay. It's the quantity of money in circulation and the $7 Trillion Federal Debt that lessens the dollar's value, and the irresponsible management of it by the Fed that should concern all of us. The Fed has triggered a world-wide "competitive devaluation" of currencies which could lead to global inflation (Chapter Ten).

As pointed out in Chapter One, after every Boom cycle there was a Bust. Every Boom going back to 1929 and the start of the Great Depression was marked by "tight money." That is, the Fed, sensing that the economy was overheating and inflation was manifesting itself, began to decrease the supply of money in the banking system and raised interest rates. Loans were more difficult to get, and the cost was much higher. As we witnessed in the past, the economy would cool, and the most severe excesses and speculation that caused the imbalance in the economy would moderate.

The Bust cycle of 1990 (when the commercial real estate market tanked) warranted extreme intervention by the Fed. The commercial banks and savings and loans that were subject to their oversight were the primary real property lenders during the boom. Congress, at the behest of the Fed, enacted the Financial Institution Reform Recovery and Enforcement Act (FIRREA) in 1987 (See Chapter One), and member banks could not make any real estate loans for a period of three years. The Boom, needless to say, came to a screeching halt—and 747 banks and savings and loans went out of business. The Federal Deposit Insurance Corp (FDIC) didn't have sufficient funds to pay off depositors in cash, and the Federal Budget deficit was out of control. Those were desperate days, but the point is that when the smoke cleared, the excesses and speculation in real estate development were quickly rung out of the market place. The write down of property values and the write off of loans was the greatest since the Great Depression. Taxpayer cost was $160 *billion*. I survived to tell this story.

The property referred to as Lincoln Resorts & Scottsdale Lakes Golf Club in Chapter One was assembled from 1983 to 1986 and was re-zoned from single family residential to a multi-use commercial property for a 500-room, 5-Star resort, golf course, and 200 residential units. This was a major feat in itself, given the location in the heart of Scottsdale, Arizona. In 1980 dollars the development cost would have been well in excess of $100,000,000 plus the cost of the land.

By 1987 it was obvious to my partner and I as well as our advisors that the boom would soon be over; and, in fact, we sold the land and entitlements at the top of the market in September 1987. The buyer assumed our underlying $8,000,000 land loan with the provision that it be paid off within two years. We carried our equity in the sale to be paid from the buyer's construction loan. Our buyer paid off our land loan just prior to the enactment of FIRREA on August 4, 1989. Unable to finance the construction of the project, our buyer defaulted on the note.

My partner and I also owned a residentially-zoned parcel adjacent to the proposed golf course which we wanted to improve and sell to builders in lots. The location was primo. On the day we paid off our loan to Merabank we met with the president of the bank. It seemed to us to be a reasonable request to borrow $3,000,000 on the residential parcel after paying off the $8,000,000 loan. The president was gracious and thanked us for performing as agreed on their loan but stated regretfully that his bank wouldn't be in a position to make the development loan. I sensed something significant was about to happen.

When we reached the lobby (we couldn't talk because bank employees were in the elevator) my partner, a savvy and experienced developer who had been in the business for 30 years, asked:

"I can't understand why they can't make the loan."

I replied, "It's over!"

"What's over?"

"I'll bet they're closing their doors. The whole game is over," I opined.

"How in the world could you come to that conclusion?" my partner replied in some disbelief.

It <u>was</u> over—my instincts were correct. The real estate boom had ended, and the hyper-inflated, absurdly appraised and over-leveraged real estate market all over the entire U.S. was forcibly re-valued. The Resolution Trust Corp. liquidated choice properties at a fraction of their previously appraised or loan value. Our land, which we sold at $13/sq. ft. in 1987, was auctioned by the RTC and resold for $4/sq. ft.—a mark-down of 75% in a period of a few years on one of the choicest pieces of dirt in Scottsdale. The nation was in a true recession from 1990 to 1994.

Personally, it was a humbling and costly experience ... but also a life-changing event. My objective was to ascertain why this meltdown occurred. What were the dynamics that caused the boom and then the bust? You, the reader, are the beneficiary of my search. I was prepared for the next cycle, and Olivia and I profited handsomely. I want you to do the same. There will be another opportunity ahead to acquire real property at a significant discount.

Other events were occurring at this same time which should have been a signal that all was not well in the entire U.S. economy. When I sold my insurance and securities operation in 1978 and became fully engaged in real estate development, I was not involved in retail security sales, which makes this story even more remarkable. I was however, watching over our investments. On Thursday, October 15, 1987, I informed Olivia:

"Honey, I'm liquidating all our equity investments today. I sense that the market is going to tank. The mutual fund company that holds your IRA requires a written authorization. I want you to sign it so I can overnight it today."

"I don't want to do that! You've told me time and time again we're in the market for the long term," Olivia responded, flippantly echoing my previous philosophy.

"Sign it!" I demanded.

You know the rest of the story. Our funds were sold on Friday and the DJIA lost 108 points, or 4%. Then the Dow lost 22.6% of its value on Monday, October 19th, the largest one-day drop in history. Five hundred billion dollars in value evaporated *in one day*! The selloff continued on Tuesday, and our large cap mutual funds would have lost 40% of their value in one week.

The stock market mania *du jour* of 1986 and 1987 was fueled by hostile takeovers, leveraged buyouts, and mergers. Superman of the era was Michael Milken who, working for Drexel Burnham, Lambert, made high-yield "junk bonds" (unrated debt securities of U.S. corporations) palatable and the source of capital that fueled the mania. The cost of funds for these deals was often 15% or more, but no one bothered to pencil it out to determine if the deal made sense. Conflict of interest, insider trading, and fraud resulted in numerous arrests and convictions finally ending one of the seediest episodes on Wall Street. Milken and others served jail time. The era became known as "The Decade of Greed," but in magnitude and impact it pales in comparison with the pervasive scope of the collateralized debt obligations (CDOs) which is the New Economy's "junk bonds."

One of Phoenix's most recognizable entrepreneurs was Karl Eller, who built a local billboard company into a media empire but lost out in a battle for control of Gannett Co. Eller, swept up in the merger mania of this era, acquired Circle K Corp. The funding came from the sale of "junk bonds." At a party celebrating Circle K's entry into the high-profile deal arena, my real estate partner had an opportunity to engage Mr. Eller in conversation that went something like this:

"I guess congratulations are in hand, Karl, but there's one thing I don't understand," my partner stated.

"What's that?" Eller replied.

"Fifteen percent interest. How in the world can a company that works off such a small gross margin pay 15% on all that debt?" he continued.

"You're right, my friend. You <u>don't</u> understand," Eller remanded his inquisitor as he engaged a more ardent admirer.

What did the deal-maker who would soon experience Circle K's collapse and bankruptcy intend to communicate?

Was it that it was the making of the deal that was relevant and nothing else mattered?

Was that an acknowledgment that he knew that the debt would never be paid?

Who knows? Maybe the answer is revealed in Eller's book, "Integrity is All You've Got." Even good people get pilloried when they succumb to manias and delusions. Don't be one of them.

Fast forward and back to the Fall of 2002. A recession was looming, but it never happened. For the first time in modern U.S. economic history (since 1929) there wasn't a recession. There was a titanic shift in strategy by the Federal Reserve that is best explained by Addison Wiggin in his book "The Demise of the Dollar":

The U.S. recession of 2001 was the mildest in postwar history. Normally in a downturn in the economy, people take stock of their personal balance sheets, pare back, pay off a little debt, and get their ducks in a row. Not so in 2001. In fact, Americans pulled out their credit cards and continued to spend their way right through the recession—so much so that the real work that generally takes place in a recession never happened. Debts didn't get paid off. Bad loans didn't get written off. The recession, rather than simply being the mildest in the postwar period, never really happened.

But we have kept ourselves in the dark, convinced that economic recovery is strong because "they" have told us so. But realistically, remain in the dark. Real GDP declined just 0.6 percent, well below the average 2 percent decline of previous postwar recession. The great question, of course, is, what actually made this recession so mild? Quoting the chairman of the Federal Reserve, Alan Greenspan: "The mildness and brevity of the downtown are a testament to the notable improvements in the resilience and flexibility of the U.S. economy."

This position—that the U.S. economy is <u>resilient</u> or <u>flexible</u>—is a widespread view among American economists. It needs drastic revision because, well, the assumption itself is absolutely false. The 2001 recession <u>was</u> unusually mild, but this positive sign was more than offset by exceptionally weak economic growth in the two years following this recession—and they don't like to talk about that.

In economics, everything is compared. We measure good and bad compared to how good or bad the averages have been. This is reasonable, or else we wouldn't know what to think about 2 percent, 8 percent, or 194 percent. In the case of the elusive and misleading (but favorite) indicator, the GDP, the decline in all postwar recessions has averaged 2 percent. But this average loss has always been followed by vigorous recoveries. On average, over the three years of recession and recovery, there is typically an average net GDP growth of 8.2 percent. Now let's compare: Over the three years 2001-2003, covering recession and recovery, real GDP grew only 5.7 percent. So any boast about a particularly mild recession, not to mention our economy's extraordinary resilience and flexibility, is an exaggeration.

*This talk about the economy's resilience and flexibility is inaccurate for still another reason. Recessions were always periods of sharply slower debt growth and repayment, reflecting retrenchment in spending. **The 2001 recession, in contrast, was a period of debt growth accelerated** (emphasis added), and that is precisely what the Greenspan Fed wanted to achieve. In* *a speech on March 4, 2003, in Orlando, Florida, Greenspan bragged about the fact that consumers had extracted huge amounts of previously build-up equities from owner-occupied homes. For the economy, such equity extraction was financed by _debt_.*

The problem has only worsened since 2001. Consumer borrowing has been growing at record annual rates. As of the end of 2004, total consumer debt ended up over $2.1 trillion, a 23 percent increase over four years.

Annual consumer spending and borrowing continue to rage higher at an annual rate of $480.3 billion. Even so, Greenspan, has pointed to consumer trends as positive indicators. That strengthening trend, however, has come from inflating stock and house prices. Debt is soaring, and _that_ is the problem. It would be different if that spending was going into a savings and retirement account or, in the case of business, into factory machinery. But it is not. The GDP growth involves spending money _and_ borrowing the money rather than using earnings. That's where the problem lie, and that's where the demise of the dollar is going to occur. At some point in the near future, our country is simply going to run out of credit. We're going to max out our monetary credit card.

It is the debt itself, out of control and getting worse, that is going to cause the loss of the dollar's spending power. The higher our consumer debt and our government debt, the weaker the dollar becomes. And that means your savings and retirement account and your Social Security check are going to be worth less and less. This currency crisis is augmented by the fact that China is taking over the world economy; it is becoming the leading importer, manufacturer, and producer in the world. [2]

Wiggin's book was published in 2005. The case he makes has been reinforced by events that have actually happened since then. Wiggin has identified "The Greenspan Plan," which asked Americans to dig themselves a deeper debt hole to get the bankers out of the one they were already in. There was no significant write down and write off of debt as there had been in every past bust cycle. Debt increased. It truly *was* different this time. The same *modus operandi* would occur in the Fall of 2007, as we'll soon discuss.

There is one other significant difference in the 1990 bust versus the one we are currently experiencing. The commercial banks and the S&Ls were the primary lenders in 1990, and they and their shareholders took direct hits as 747 went out of business. The current list of lenders is primarily a lightly regulated mortgage industry that originates the loans and sells them off to Wall Street or various government-sponsored enterprises (GSEs) such as Fannie Mae or Freddie Mac, who both have recently had their own financial fiasco. Some real estate investment trusts (REITs) like New Century Financial retained the subprime loans, and they're already bankrupt. A clever move by the Federal banks to avoid a revisit to the dire days of 1990. But *Greed* gave the MOD a new opportunity they couldn't resist—Collateralized Debt Obligations (CDOs).

Chapter Four
A Modern Mania
(Tulips to Daisies)

In the Preface I referred to Charles MacKay's timeless treatise, "Extraordinary Popular Delusions & the Madness of Crowds" written in 1841. It's a worthy exercise to revisit the fallibility of the consensus and apply what we should have already known to contemporary events.

"Tulip Mania" is a term often heard when the blast of hot air is released from a bursting economic bubble. What could have been the virtue or the unique qualities of a flower to have made it so valuable in the eyes of such a prudent, practical, and financially astute people as the Dutch? By the mid-17th Century, the reputation of the tulip increased "until it was deemed a proof of bad taste for any man of fortune to be without a collection of them," said MacKay. He adds, "In 1634, the rage among the Dutch to possess them was so great that the ordinary industry of the country was neglected—and the population, even to its lowest dregs, embarked in the tulip trade."

The tulip became more valuable than gold bullion. Eventually the rich people were no longer willing to pay the exorbitant price for the flower, and speculators and dealers who had contracted to buy and sell the bulbs for fixed prices began to default. A panic ensued. Within a short period tulips that had sold for 6,000 florins were worth 500, or a drop of 90%. Tulip Mania could have been the seminal event that moved the Dutch to migrate to the New World and discover New Amsterdam—a city later to be renamed New York and the future origin of many "Tulip Manias."

Obviously, the product could be real estate, gold, stocks, or masterpieces of art. It matters not. It's the human condition of *Greed* that fuels all manias.

In keeping with the flower motif, there exists in our own arcane and mysterious world of finance (known only to the most sophisticated bankers and Wall Street traders) a chain of daises that ultimately will be America's version of Tulip Mania. Like the tulip traders of centuries ago who entered into contracts to guarantee the purchase and sale of tulips at a specified price, Wall Street and our banking system has amassed an incredible sum of $300 to $400 trillion in derivatives, which are guarantees to buy or sell various assets or derivatives of those assets at a specified price and at a specified point in time. This "daisy chain" is only as strong as its weakest link. Default and the inability of one or more of the guarantors (counter parties) sets in motion a chain of events that far exceeds the Fed's ability to prevent a meltdown of a magnitude that history has never previously recorded.

Author's Note:

In January, 2008, the weakest link in the derivative daisy chain snapped.

Credit-default swaps came into focus. These are swaps where one party, for a price, assumes the risk that a bank or loan will go bad. Suddenly, the real and present danger now exists that one of the parties to the millions of trades can't pay its losses. The guarantees would become worthless.

In a feature first-page article in the Wall Street Journal (January 18, 2008). [3], the journalists illuminate the story at ACA, a bond insurer who has $425 million of capital in comparison to $69 billion of credit protection. ACA, like numerous other bond insurers, will need massive amounts of new capital or the cooperation of all parties to unwind these contracts in order to avoid collapse.

In 2002, when Berkshire Hathaway, Inc. acquired General Re Corp (a reinsurer), Warren Buffet discovered that General Re had 23,218 derivative contracts on the company's books. Buffet directed the company to "pull back from the business of these swaps." It took General Re four years to unravel these complex instruments. Buffet said,

"We lost over $400 million on contracts that were supposedly safe and properly priced and we did it in a leisurely way in a benign market. If we had to unwind it in one month, who knows what would have

happened?"

Today with hundreds of billions in defaults and institutions desperately looking for a lifesaver in a whirlpool of debt, the results could be catastrophic.

Here's the key point to this issue that is not included in the Wall Street Journal article. Who was the champion and advocate for this massive $400 trillion daisy chain of derivatives? Who was the one person who defended the proliferation of these leveraged casino bets in front of Congress to prevent the government's desire to regulate the derivative industry? None other than Alan Greenspan (the enabler). This fact will become more relevant after you complete your reading of Greed.

The tale of John Law and the Mississippi Company described by MacKay is a vivid display of delusions and the madness of crowds.

France was virtually bankrupt after the death of spend-thrift and corrupt King Louis XIV in 1715. Enter John Law, a Scotsman with a scheme to save the country from ruin. Law convinced the French that their country could not prosper without a paper currency, as their medium of exchange was then gold and silver coin. Law proposed that he be permitted to form a private bank administered in the King's name which would issue paper notes payable on sight. Within a year these notes were more valuable (in the minds of the French) than the precious metal coins and carried a premium of 15% over the notes issued by the government. Basically, Law introduced a privately owned federal bank that issued a paper currency. France was soon inundated with paper money. Sound familiar?

Law, despite being a foreigner and a Protestant, capitalized further on his fame and fortune. He proposed to the government that he establish a company with the exclusive rights of trading "to the great river Mississippi and the Provence of Louisiana"—not yet a part of our United States. The sale of shares in the Mississippi Company set off a speculative frenzy never before seen in France.

Law's bank had promulgated so much good that the Regent conferred upon the bank the sole right to refine gold and silver and the exclusive monopoly of the sale of tobacco. The private bank ultimately became the Royal Bank of France and, as a public institution, "caused a fabrication of notes to the amount of one thousand million of liras," which presumably was an issue of paper far in excess of the bank's ability to have the necessary funds to provide for them. By 1720 the delusion of wealth and the rampant speculation in the shares collapsed, and Law was fortunate to escape with his life.

The United States went off the final vestiges of a gold standard in 1971 when Richard Nixon was President. Since that date there has been no link between our currency and gold and no limits as to any amount of currency we issue except what individuals and governments will extend to the U.S. in credit. We have a fiat (paper) money system. Ever since the Roman Empire, every nation that abandoned a gold standard lost control of its currency and its economy. The U.S. is now keeping that dubious record intact.

In 1992, while the U.S. was attempting to recover from the devastating real estate debacle noted earlier, Olivia and I, during our annual retreat to develop a strategy to deal with the realities of life, made a critical decision that would prove to be fortuitous.

Olivia had started her career in real estate, ironically, in 1979 when long-term mortgage interest rates were 16% and the residential market was in the toilet. Undeterred, by the mid-1980s she had established herself as one of the top luxury home agents in the Scottsdale-Paradise Valley area. Previously, she was an English professor at the college level.

My career started in the life insurance business in 1960, expanded to full financial services by the mid-60s, and morphed into a three-state brokerage operation in the 1970s. I sold my three offices at the top of the market in 1978, and Olivia and I secured our real estate licenses at the same time. In 1992 we made the decision to diversify our professions. We had our income source in one basket in the 1990 real estate collapse and the Easter Bunny left us no eggs. I returned to financial services, which proved to be a wise decision.

Phoenix, Scottsdale, and other areas in Arizona have enjoyed a vibrant and dynamic real estate market during the past twenty-five years due, in part, to a consistent population growth. Phoenix proper in 1950 had a population of 106,818. By the end of 2006 it had grown to 1,505,000 and is now the fifth largest city in the U.S. The metroplex, which consists of over 500 square miles, has approximately 3.6 million people ... a healthy market for builders and the legions of servile followers from appraisers, real estate brokers and agents, mortgage bankers, title companies, and the like. It has often been said that even when the real estate market is bad in Phoenix, it's probably better than almost anywhere else in the country.

Anecdotal evidence from Olivia's files illustrates the mania that permeated this marketplace at its top in mid-2005.

Olivia placed a home in the Multiple Listing Service (MLS) on a Friday with condition that the house could not be shown until Sunday. By early Saturday morning she received a full price offer with no contingencies other than an inspection. She finalized the sale on Monday.

Another was an older home with a large lot and a spectacular view of the city. She received three offers on the first day the property was listed, and each was over the asking price of $2,500,000. Olivia and the owner requested that the three offerees re-submit their bids and the owner would select the highest bidder. The house sold for $2,700,000. The buyer immediately tore down the older (but very livable) home and sold the land for $3,500,000.

An associate of Olivia's listed a home located in Arcadia within two miles of our residence. Within a week eleven offers were received on the house. Virtually every realtor has a similar story. "It was absolutely 'nuts'," one experienced old pro told me.

Based upon one person's success, which would also mirror that of agents all over the U.S., Olivia and her constituents should be singing the praises of Mr. Greenspan and the Fed who were principally responsible for this manic market. Most agents, however, come now not to praise Caesar but to bury him and the investment bankers who created the CDOs. And rightly so.

I often ask agents which they would prefer: a market like the one that you've just experienced with five years of extremely high sales and then what could be in the future two or three years of a dead market, or an environment where market conditions are consistent based upon supply and demand fundamentals? The seasoned professionals want consistency. The young "millennials" (Chapter Eight) want the manic market more suitable to their "me-first-now lifestyle." Most of these young lions, I suspect, won't be around to experience either.

The Fed's stated mission is to foster "a stable growth economy." We might put a number of labels on the U.S. economy during the past five years, but "stable" is not one of them.

The reader, however, shouldn't conclude that everything was 'hunky-dory' in Arizona. A recently completed study by the Corporation for Enterprise Development (CFED) gives the State of Arizona an F (failing) grade for financial prosperity, which comes as a shock to most "Zonies." (We call Californians "Left Coasters," and they call us "Zonies".)[4]

The study by CFED ranks the 50 states on 46 measures that reflect asset building, business development, health insurance, home ownership, and the like. The CFED said that Arizonans struggle with high debt burdens (ranking 49th out of 50 states for subprime loans), 38th for credit card balances, and 47th for installment debt. Bottom line, "Zonies" are not well protected from potential financial catastrophes like the one currently unfolding.

Many Arizonans will resent and reject the CFED findings. Heck, who wants an F? But the fluid, fast-paced economy and the high-energy and opportunistic lifestyle we Arizonans enjoy also breeds complacency. There is a live-for-today mentality amongst the Boomers and Generation X-ers in the state which in many cases would contribute to the F grade. Arizona also has a large retired senior population which is fiscally conservative. This group has no debt on their homes and one of the largest bank balances per depositor of any area in the U.S. It's possible that the CFED data gathers did not make it to the outer regions where Sun City, Leisure World, and other upscale retirement communities exist.

What states received an A on their report card? In the west,

Montana, Wyoming, and Hawaii were the only good students. The Midwest states of Minnesota, Wisconsin, and Iowa also made the grade. The New England states of Maine, New Hampshire, Vermont, and Massachusetts also garnered an A. The full report card can be read at www.cfed.org/go/scorecard/

What does the study prove or disprove? Probably nothing in a micro-sense to you as an individual other than those who are already a casualty. Arizonans filed 1,021 applications for bankruptcy protection in August 2007, up 65% from the same month in 2006. Nationwide there were 74,607 filings in August, up 31% from a year earlier. The CFED data which was compiled a year earlier is validated by the current rise in bankruptcies. The question is: will this trend continue, and for how long? Read on.

One could conclude, however, that the 14 states that received a D or F face the prospect of budgetary shortfalls stemming from higher social and entitlement costs and lower tax revenues. In the ensuing year or two the impact of this massive debt contraction will be felt by all U.S. taxpayers. I suspect the state of California will bear the brunt of the tax shortfall. The 2007 Deficit is estimated to be a whopping $15.6 *billion*. Will the "left coasters" terminate the Terminator? Politicians in most states, as well as the Federal government, assumed that the receipts would remain at peak levels and increased spending. Now deficits will balloon.

In retrospect, 2005 marked the top of the housing market in most areas of the U.S. The hottest of the hottest markets arguably was Naples, on Florida's West Coast. This was an upscale, quiet retirement community where the median home price doubled between 2000 and 2005 to approximately $482,400. It was also fertile ground for a Canadian transplant by the name of Marjorie Dresner, a home "flipper" of great renown. The National Association of Realtors found that nationwide, 28% of home buyers were investors. In Naples, 50% may have been investors. Marjorie was the Queen Bee, buying dozens of homes. Her story typifies this *Greed*-drawn modern mania and her fall from grace. Here are a few of her transactions:

Three-Bedroom Lakefront Home

February, 2001 Sales Price	$275,000
July, 2005 Dresner & Partner Purchase Price	$690,000
High Bid at October, 2006 Auction	$400,000

Duplex

April, 2005 Sales Price	$347,000
October, 2005 Dresner & Partner Purchase Price	$621,000
High Bid at October, 2006 Auction	$250,000

Three-Bedroom Lakefront Home

October, 2002 Sales Price	$200,000
September, 2004 Dresner Purchase Price	$435,000
High Bid at October, 2006 Auction	$275,000

Sources: J. J. Manning Auctioneers; Collier Co., FCA Records, Wall Street Journal January 8, 2007.

Ms. Dresner's losses on these three properties were more than 50% of her purchase price. What the Wall Street Journal article does not report, however, is what actual loss, if any, did she incur? Were these "No-Doc" loans that required no cash down payment? How many monthly payments did Ms. Dresner make? Did the lender absorb all of the loss? We don't know. She may even have laughed her way to the bank after the auctions.

Typically, nationwide where speculators, investors, flippers, or whatever appropriate designation you may want to use plied their trade, they simply walked from their obligation and let the chips fall where they may. Did the lenders get their just desserts for making irrational loans? Is it fair that speculators pocket their profits when their timing is right and don't incur any personal loss when it isn't? And what about the "moral hazard" which provides a safety net for speculators of all stripes knowing there's a bailout to cover their loss which encourages the risk-taker to do it all over again? We'll revisit this question later.

There are some notable twists to the Dresner story.

A real estate broker met Ms. Dresner when he sold her his own home for $435,000, more than double what he paid for it. Two years later Ms. Dresner defaulted, and the home sold at auction to the highest bidder. The price? $275,000. The buyer? The same real estate broker re-purchased his former home. "It would have been stupid not to bid," the buyer said to the reporters.

Some of the quotes from the deposed "flipper queen" are priceless. Ms. Dresner says in the Wall Street Journal article that she never bought a home for more than its appraised value and "I never overpaid for anything." As both Countrywide Home Loans, Inc. and the Bank of New York filed papers to foreclose on two other properties owned by Ms. Dresner, she reportedly said that she isn't in financial difficulty. It appears that Ms. Dresner is trying to convince the reader (and herself) that she hasn't lost any money. You know what's ludicrous? Maybe she didn't.

In December of 2005, prior to my retirement from financial services, a young man was referred to me by his accountant. He was 28 years old, had a family, was on fast track to becoming a multi-millionaire, and desperately needed planning. During the fact-finding interview I discovered that he and his family were living in one home that he built to sell while building another to move into when his present home sold. His firm, for which he was the designated broker and responsible for a number of real estate agents, had also subdivided and improved lots for sale to builders or investors. He was also buying land for his own account. He was totally immersed in a feeding frenzy as his cell phone rang five times during a forty-five minute interview.

His accountant wanted the man to set up a qualified retirement plan and fund the maximum amount to reduce his tax liability in 2005. To cut to the chase, despite our follow-up and his accountant's persistence, the plan and numerous other recommendations were never acted upon (he did buy a Hummer). Unfortunately for him and his family, those funds that would have been set aside in the qualified plan would have been free from creditor's rights and may have helped him recover from the inevitable crash that burst his bubble.

It was, in many respects, *deja vu* all over again. I had the experience and the wisdom of the 1990 contraction in the real estate market that others could benefit from, but many took Yogi Berra's advice, "when you get to a fork in the road, take it."

Armed with a considerable amount of new-found knowledge, I began teaching a Continuing Education class at the Southwestern School of Real Estate in Scottsdale entitled "Real Estate Cycles & Trends." Here is a brief piece that I wrote in 1994 introducing my class:

REAL ESTATE CYCLES AND TRENDS

In the fall of 1992, the real estate market in the Valley, as well as nationally, was still in the doldrums. We had all just witnessed and experienced the largest contraction of real estate values since the Great Depression and to say brokers and agents were optimistic relative to the future would be a gross misrepresentation.

I taught my first real estate class in November, 1992, and informed a skeptical audience that the Valley was about to experience one of the biggest residential and multi-family booms ever beginning in 1993 and 1994. I use the same transparency today that I used in that first class, because my original assessment was accurate. Did I have a crystal ball, clairvoyance or voice mail access to Nostradamus? None of the above! What I did have, however, were hard facts, experience, and the ability to spot major shifts in economic cycles and trends. Here is what I knew that most agents, developers and builders didn't focus on:

1.   The Financial Institution Reform Recovery and Enforcement Act (FIRREA) enacted by Congress in 1989 which severely limited banks from making real estate loans was due to expire on December 31, 1992.

2.   Alan Greenspan's plan to restore financial health to the nation's banks by requiring the banks to borrow from the Federal Reserve bank at artificially low rates and using the funds to buy U.S. Treasury debt had produced the desired result. As interest rates continued to decline, however, the banks' margin or spread was shrinking, so the banks would have both the capital and the incentive to make real estate loans.

3.   The Fifth Migration (people moving away from congested cities and suburbs) was underway, and the migration from California to Arizona would positively impact our market.

4.   Low interest rates would stimulate all markets—stocks and bonds as well as real estate.

5.   "Smart money" was buying multi-family units and raw land at bargain basement prices, a strong contrarian market indicator of positive future activity.

Reliable information, particularly in advance of major market shifts, is invaluable. Some apartment investors who bought units in 1992 (24,000 units sold) and earlier have realized gains of 100% or more by 1994. Those agents and brokers who worked the residential market vigorously during the lean years reaped the benefits as the buyer's market of 1993 became the seller's market of 1994.

So, what's ahead? First, look to the past to see the future. The Valley real estate market for the three years 1993 through 1995 could prove to be very similar to the years 1977 through 1979. In 1977 the Valley, as well as the nation, was emerging from a "soft" real estate market of the mid-1970s due to Nixon's resignation, the oil crisis, and a tight money supply. During the three year period beginning in 1977, sales of all forms of real estate in the Valley were spectacular. In addition, price increases enjoyed one of the largest percentage increases ever. However, by 1980 the prime rate had risen to 21.5%, and 30-year fixed rate mortgages were 15%. A neologism was born—STAGFLATION. That robust cycle was over, and with it went the dreams and dollars of many who didn't read the signs.

Fast forward to today (1994). Is it deja vu all over again? Are we experiencing a period of low inflation and low interest rates today followed by a trend towards much higher numbers? There is a huge GAP between the perception that conditions will continue to remain as they are and the reality that they will change. Those who look for that GAP will profit because the environment exists for the next cycle to be more pronounced than the previous one.

I begin my class with the statement that we're living in the midst of the greatest social, political, technological, and economic revolution since the 1930s, which in itself makes it difficult to see. The fortunes of the real estate market will always be vulnerable to the economics of change. The key is knowledge, because knowledge is the secret to wealth. Remember, it wasn't raining when Noah built the ark.

Fast forward further to May 2005. The owners of the Southwestern School of Real Estate and I thought it was appropriate, given the dynamics of the marketplace, to hold a special seminar for both homeowners and agents. Agents were in a bind because they didn't have any listings. Homeowners were perplexed by what was happening all around them and needed fresh ideas. From this situation came a pregnant idea. Here is an excerpt from pages 31 to 33:

THE REAL ESTATE OPPORTUNITY OF A LIFETIME

The following letter was written by a retiree to TAIPAN, a financial newsletter to which I subscribe:

"I'm a retired engineer, 77 years old, but still strongly active, who is trying to get by on a very meager portfolio given today's high cost living and low, low fixed income yields (of reasonable safety). I recently talked with a local financial consultant who said that 50% of the people who live on Cape Cod are financially strapped, retired people whose homes (which have tripled and quadrupled in value in the last 10 years) are their main asset and, in many cases, mortgaged to meet living needs. But even the rest of the U.S. (probably including Maryland) has a huge population, many not even retired, who have mortgaged their homes and will be in disaster when (not if) that last bubble bursts. So guys, how about a very serious and very pertinent play: a hedge on the house? Can (you) work out a feasible strategy? I will stay eagerly tuned in for the next episode."

Based upon my (H. L. Quist) extensive experience working and consulting with people who are age 50 or over, many of them have a similar story:

•   They've lived in their present home for a considerable period of time. It's debt free or nearly so. Their home has appreciated 300% to 500% in the past 20 years with much of the increase coming in the past three years.

•   Their home is their largest asset but they don't (and shouldn't) want to borrow on their equity.

•   Their invested assets produce extremely low returns and remain at risk.

•   Social Security is their principal source of income. They realize that their cost of living has increased dramatically and they feel the "squeeze" that most Americans are experiencing at all ages.

•   They are not aware of the $500,000 capital gains exclusion on the sale of their home. (Only 16% respondents could identify these tax benefits according to CCH Complete Tax.) Go to www.irs.gov publication 523 for complete tax information. A revision of the IRS Tax Code is high on the President's agenda.

It is time to consider:

DOWNSIZE YOUR HOME <u>NOW</u> AND
SECURE YOUR FINANCIAL FUTURE

The sale of your home and moving to a new location is an emotional as well as a financial decision. Consider a few possibilities:

•   Pay cash for a smaller home or condo. A family member recently sold his house that had an existing loan and purchased a similar-sized home for cash in Green Valley, Arizona. Relocating outside metro-Phoenix provides an opportunity to financially downsize without giving up space and comfort.

•   Move to a senior multi-care type facility. Maybe the time is right to make this move and enjoy the opportunity to meet new friends.

•   Rent a home. When the bubble bursts there will be an oversupply of investor-owned homes for rent at rock-bottom rates. The May 27, 2005 issue of the Wall Street Journal had a feature article entitled,

"For Homeowners, It's All In The Timing." One story told is that of Herb and Nicki Brown in Long Beach, California, who are in their seventies and sold their home for almost twice its purchase price five years prior. Herb plans to rent for one year until he retires to move to Phoenix. The couple lived in Victorville, California in the 1980s and saw the value of their home drop 40% in one year. He didn't want to see that happen again. Herb was right. It was probably his last opportunity of a lifetime where he could pocket a $300,000 tax free cash gain.

   • *Consider a sale and lease back of your own home. There are a wealth of investors who firmly believe that your home is going to continue to skyrocket in value and want to offset a portion of their debt service. Maybe, just maybe, you'll be able to buy your home back at a sizeable discount later.*

   • *Travel. Buy a motor home and tour the USA. A client of my wife's bought a boat and sailed around the world. Be adventurous and live a little.*

   • *Buy a home in Costa Rica or another country. A friend purchased a home on the beach in Costa Rica for $65,000 and his cost of living is a fraction of what it was in Phoenix. There has been a mass migration of Americans and Canadians to Costa Rica.*

   • *Move in with the kids! Don't laugh. If the times really get tough they may need to share expenses.*

What may have been received in 2005 as radical ideas are now, in hindsight to many in 2007, an opportunity lost. Immediately comes to mind the agent who sold Ms. Dresner his home in Naples, Florida. He pocketed over $200,000 profit in 2004 and bought his home back at auction for about $50,000 more than he paid for it. Review my suggestion above (consider a sale and lease back of your own home), where I projected, "Maybe, just maybe, you'll be able to buy back your home at a sizeable discount." There is an advantage to living a long time and having your synapses still firing.

   While writing this book, I have asked the agents attending my class, "How many of you have senior customers, family, or friends who took advantage of this opportunity before the market correction started?" A few, possibly 10% to 20%, raise their hands. Then I ask, "How many of these same folks wish they had sold their homes?" The response is almost always 70% to 80%. Incredibly, many of these seniors who now realize an opportunity lost admit that their reason for not selling was they thought their home would bring a higher price if they waited. Remember the axiom:

When markets are at the top of a boom cycle, no one thinks they'll ever end.

When markets are at the bottom of a bust cycle, no one thinks they'll ever get better.

The (MOD) had a very appealing, albeit misleading, advertising campaign. The hardest sale to make to a person is death insurance. It only benefits the beneficiary. The easiest sale to make to a person is to appeal to their *Greed*. What will the product or service do for them? The enormous success (if you can call mass indenture a success) of the REFI phenomena was in large part an appeal to the homeowner's *Greed*. Between 2002 and 2006 a *trillion dollars* was refinanced, and it is estimated that a large percentage of that amount generated cash and tax-free money to the borrower. In retrospect, *Greed* won out over reason and fear:

BE DEBT FREE!

Variations of the same theme were to refinance the home, pay off credit cards and other short-term debt, and take cash out to spend the "free" money at the borrower's pleasure. The "teaser" ARM or interest-only loan in most cases significantly lowered the monthly debt service. Homeowners ignored the fact that their total debt was, at the closing, greater than prior to their refinancing. In some cases some probably convinced themselves that they were out of debt. By summer 2007, as the subprime mortgage mess began to unfold, these homeowners discovered first hand that not only were they not debt free, the lunch was also not free.

Debt free was an illusion, of course. How do we know? The Federal Trade Commission (FTC) in September 2007 filed its first charges against lenders for "misleading advertising." If the FTC is successful and they are able to collect fines from any solvent lenders, quite possibly some of these funds may be returned to homeowners. The real question is, why didn't they take action sooner? The FTC must have pressed the mute button on the MOD's advertising.

The Federal Regulators have also determined that many MODs violated Truth In Lending Rules. By late 2007, the Fed had also proposed new rules regarding advertising. Why weren't these rule changes made in 2005?

Cheap, and a seemingly inexhaustible supply of money available to anyone with a pulse fueled this real estate mania never before experienced in America. Though denied by virtually everyone in the real estate and lending industry, the U.S. was in a bubble. The only question was, would it suddenly "pop"—or would the speculative air "fizzle out" over a of couple of years?

There is a subtle but key issue that separates the New Economy from the Old Economy that truly makes today's mortgage meltdown "different this time."

In the olden days your banker was often your financial counselor. You had, often times, a close personal relationship with your banker, and he was not only concerned that his loan to you would be repaid ... he didn't want you, the borrower, to be placed in a position of duress where your business and family could be impaired. Collateral and the economic sense of the deal were factors, of course, but your personal character and reputation to make good on your obligation was a paramount consideration. Quite often, your banker turned down your loan because it wasn't right for you at that moment in time.

In the New Economy and under the guidelines (real or imagined) promulgated by the Greenspan Plan of 2002, bankers abandoned *out-of-date* underwriting principles. Character wasn't a consideration any more. Non-payment of debt was not a primary concern. The goal was to commoditize as much debt as possible, accepting the prospect of a higher default rate as an incremental cost of doing business. Many bankers became impersonal Merchants of Debt. The concept of banking in the New Economy will undergo a severe stress test in 2008.

Rachel Beck of the Associated Press reported on November 7, 2007,[5] that "many of the Nation's big banks and credit card companies have begun acknowledging that they are seeing a shift in consumer behavior, including more people unable to pay off their debts."

Capital One Financial Corp. boosted its estimate for credit losses next year to $5 billion for its credit cards. Citigroup reported that cardholders are taking cash advances for the first time. Credit card debt of $17.3 billion is now 30 days past due, and defaults are at $1 trillion. The credit contagion is spreading, thanks to aggressive marketing by the Merchants of Debt. Even American Express, which is considered the Cadillac of credit cards because it has a more creditworthy and sophisticated customer base, reported a dramatic increase in delinquencies in December 2007. When defaults were running 2% to 3% of the companies' outstanding balances, the credit card companies had little concern because their profit margin was so high. Now delinquencies have doubled with the prospect of double-digit defaults in the near future. Bankers haven't realized yet that most of the credit card outstanding debt will <u>never be paid</u>.

Chapter Five
Subprime Goes Prime Time
(The Meltdown Begins)

There is much truth in fables, despite our parents' remonstration that we shouldn't fib or "tell fables." An updated version of the "Three Little Pigs" serves a purpose.

Once upon a time there were three little pigs, and the time came for them to leave home and seek their fortune. Before they left, their mother told them, "Whatever you do, be sure to build your home out of good materials in a good location, so it will be safe and your house will appreciate in value."

The first little pig built his house out of straw bales (a new technology) because it was cheap and it was easy to build.

The second little pig built his house out of cheap wood and drywall, because it looked good and he could flip it for a nice profit.

The third little pig built his house out of bricks, despite the fact that it was more expensive and it required the pig to put a large mortgage on his house.

One day a big bad wolf, who was a real estate speculator, came along and saw the first piggie in his house of straw bales. He said, "Let me in, let me in little pig. I want to buy your house."

"Not by the hair of my chinny chin chin," said the little pig.

Unable to make a deal for the little pig's house, the big bad wolf huffed and puffed until he blew the house down and later he bought the lot for a pittance.

The wolf also tried to buy the second piggie's house made of cheap wood and drywall, but again he was rebuffed by, "Not by the hair of my chinny chin chin."

Again the big bad wolf huffed and puffed until he blew the house down and later bought the lot for a fraction of its cost.

Then the big bad wolf came to the beautiful and expensive brick home and knocked on the door. "Let me in, let me in," the big bad wolf said. "I want to buy your house."

"Not by the hair of my chinny chin chin," the wiser but over-leveraged pig replied.

The equally wise old wolf knew that all his huffing and puffing wouldn't bring down the well-built brick house. He decided against an entry down the chimney (that led to his demise in the original fable), and contemplated a different strategy.

"No need to huff and puff," the wolf thought. "I'll just wait until the real estate market collapses and the piggie's bank repos the house." Lo and behold, he was right and he bought the house at auction.

And what happened to the three little pigs? They moved back in with their mom and received compensation from the government for their loss. They, like so many homeowners, got swallowed up by the housing mania ... but at least they weren't eaten alive by the big bad wolf as told in the original fable.

This yarn may elicit a little chuckle, but obviously we're talking about real people here, not cloven-hoofed mammals. Without question there's personal tragedy in this whole real property story which mutes the humor, but the pig as a symbol of gluttony plays a major role as this tale unfolds.

Since the focus of **Greed** is its impact on the "Middle Class" in America, an attempt to define the various socio-economic classes is a difficult but necessary process.

Sociologists Dennis Gilbert, William Thompson, Joseph Hickey, and James Henslin have outlined a class system with six distinct social classes[6].

They are:

Class	% of Total Population*	Occupation	Compensation
Capitalist/Elite	1	Top Executives, Celebrities & Heirs	$500,000 +
Upper Middle	15	Professionals & Middle Management	$100,00 to $499,000
Lower Middle	30	Semi-Professional & Craftsmen	$35,000 to $75,000
Working Class	30	Clerical & Blue Collar	$16,000 to $35,000
Working Poor	13	Service, Clerical & some Blue Collar	$18,000 typical
Under Class	12	Not employed or reliant on Government Assistance	—

*Rounded.

Missing from this Academic Model is a 'class' which could be referred to as the Middle-Middle Class ($75,000 to $100,000). It appears that virtually all classes (with the possible exception of the Elite) were participants in the mortgage meltdown. Initially it was thought that subprime lending only occurred within the lower-middle and the working classes. Current data (as of October 2007), however, reveals that subprime lending took place within 99% of the U.S. population, which is compelling anecdotal evidence why the mortgage meltdown is so pervasive.

Real estate agents often ask me, "How are you able to determine so far in advance that this market is going to change?" Or, "How did you know in July 2005 that the boom would soon end?"

It's quite easy, and you don't have to possess the powers of Nostradamus. You:

1. Read what the experts are saying outside your industry, and
2. Understand the human condition and man's history of

illusions.

The purpose of *Greed* is to give you an historic perspective of economic cycles.

Unfortunately, few read what the experts were saying, particularly when it interfered with their own mind set and shed a negative light on their own perspective. And mass euphoria (or its dreaded symbiotic sister, fear) fogs the faculties of the human condition. Case in point:

As early in the boom as August 24, 2004, James Bovard wrote a feature op-ed piece in Barron's entitled, "Nothing Down, The Bush Administration's Wrecking Ball Benevolence." Bovard wrote:

"One of the proudest elements of President Bush's 'compassionate conservative' agenda has been financial support to homeowners for down payments. Bush is determined to end the bias against people who want to buy a home but don't have any money. But he is exposing taxpayers to tens of billions of dollars of possible losses, luring thousands of moderate-income families into bankruptcy, and risking the destruction of entire neighborhoods." [7]

You'll recall that the American Down Payment Dream Act $10,000 handout mentioned earlier was passed by Congress in 2003. The President not only borrowed a page from President Lyndon Johnson's Great Society play book, he opened the door for mortgage companies to the plethora of nothing-down programs to follow. Bovard's focus was to highlight this piece of legislation, but the fallout that he forecasted was magnified with the no-down mania that followed. So where did the lenders get their "directive" to expand this altruistic but flawed program? From President Bush and Congress, of course. Since the election was approaching, it was just another example of a program designed for short-term political gain that would result in a long-term financial disaster ... an American tradition.

Bovard highlights several other issues that illuminate what is occurring at the end of 2007.

The Bush administration knew or should have known that in 2002,

12% of all Federal Housing Administration (FHA) mortgages to moderate-income homeowners were past due. Between 1996 and 2000, 21% of FHA borrowers in low-income areas in Baltimore had defaulted, and 25% of FHA borrowers in the New York City borough of Queens had defaulted. The National Journal said in 1971 that the FHA was "financing the collapse of large residential areas in the center of cities." So historically, we had been there and done that.

Bovard maintains that "They (the borrowers) are worse off than if they had never received assistance." What is the psychological impact of losing your home? It has to be devastating. So what has been gained in this short-term euphoric boom cycle? Nothing, except it has created massive fee income for the MOD including, in particular, those who packaged the loans and sold them to suckers who had little or no comprehension of what they bought. More later.

Perhaps the premier prognostication that advanced his view of the U.S. housing boom (and certainly made this writer a convert) was Yale University economist Robert Shiller. Shiller had written a best seller, "Irrational Exuberance," predicting a bear market in U.S. stocks. It was released in March 2000, less than a week before the NASDAQ began its 75% decline which bottomed in the fall of 2002. My first book *"Secrets, A Novel of Golf & Politics"* also hit the market at the same time. Although the focus of "Secrets" was political, my fictional hero also forecasted a major decline in the stock market. When Shiller spoke everyone should have listened ... but few did.

Shiller's conclusion early in mid-year 2005 was "The [real estate] market is in the throes of a bubble of unprecedented proportions that probably will end ugly."[8] We probably haven't reached ugly yet—but the baby is not very good looking! Shiller also took a poke at a glib fundamental explanation offered by housing bulls to justify home prices' "moonshot." The running of the bulls was represented by none other than David Lereach, Chief Economist for the National Association of Realtors (NAR), who wrote "Are you Missing the Real Estate Boom? Why home Values and Other Real Estate Investments will Climb Through the End of the Decade—and How to Profit from Them." It's difficult to see how the publisher could fit the entire title on the cover, but there's little doubt as to the message. Question is, how could one economist be so accurate and one be so far from reality that he must have suffered from fecalopia?

What message would you expect an economist for NAR to deliver to Realtors®? He's a minister preaching to his flock ... a coach firing up his charges ... a sales manager fortifying his minions to ignore naysayers. David Lereach knows from where the adulation and his remuneration was and is derived. And there's no one now who cares to point out his absurd point of view. Hey, there's nothing disingenuous about trying to stimulate sales, but there are mines that were planted in that reality—and it's up to you to discover them before they explode. When the super hype is transmitted to you, the buyer or the seller, you have to step back and separate fact from fiction. Irrational exuberance might be desirous in the bedroom, but it can have a calamitous result for you as an investor in the markets. Cold and calculating works well when money is the medium.

Shiller made the following observations at the height of the boom:

- Flipping condos demonstrates that "tulipmania" reigns.
- A real price decline as much as 50% is U.S. home prices could occur over the next decade.
- A recession could prick the bubble, or prices could simply crash under their own weight.
- Many of the innovations in home finance may ultimately destroy the bubble they helped create.
- The housing bubble is a product of manic shifts in mass psychology.

Shiller's analysis of the U.S. housing market was amazingly astute two years later. Economists normally never stick their neck out more than 90 days and avoid at all costs being wrong. Millions of people could have profited from this information; but unfortunately, those who should read, don't. You are an exception. (Shiller later developed the S&P/Case-Shiller

Home Price Index.)

How could agents in my C.E. class have benefitted from this information when I spoke to them in 2005? While in the midst of the greatest real property market in history it seemed prudent to me that agents should be stashing away commission dollars into a rainy-day fund and tax deferring the maximum allowable into qualified retirement plans. To my knowledge very few seized the opportunity, convinced the market would continue unabated and they would set up a plan "later." Unfortunately, in my work with agents for the past fifteen years, only a few have grasped the concept that they must pay themselves first.

During this period agents, title companies, mortgage companies, and the like were expanding exponentially—particularly mortgage brokers. It was time to resist that temptation to open new offices and hire and train new people. Many signed five-year leases and personally guaranteed the obligation. Within 18 months the offices were closed, and the lease payments are continuing. The rule is simply this: when the markets are the most manic and you can't find your bottom with two hands, it's time to prepare for a shift. If you can't handle all the calls, split the business with an associate or cherry-pick the lucrative business and decline the remainder.

Denial is not a river in Egypt. Shiller's interview outlined above was aggressively attacked by Neil Barasky in the Wall Street Journal on 7-28-05 with an op-ed piece entitled "What Housing Bubble?" Taking the opposite but majority view at the time, Barasky maintained that the U.S. housing market had a "serious shortage and affordability crisis," but there was no bubble.

Barasky puts forth arguments that deny various myths advanced by those whom he termed "housing bubble Chicken Littles." Rather than dwell on one man's numbers vs. another's (because we know anyone can find numbers to support their position), it's what Barasky *didn't* say that's noteworthy. He said, "I am now a money manager. I currently own stocks in several home builders, so I am putting my money where my mouth is."

Thanks to my friends at Strategic Investment, Barasky, who manages Alson Partners LLC, was on record for the following:

1.   Mr. Barasky writes a letter for the Wall Street Journal proclaiming there is no real estate bubble.

2.   Mr. Barasky calls housing bears "Chicken Littles."

3.   Mr. Barasky says, "I am putting my money where my mouth is."

4.   Mr. Barasky is managing partner of Alson Capital Partners, LLC.

5.   Alson Capital Partners, LLC sold 896,680 shares of Toll Brothers (TOC), a major home builder, in the first quarter of 2005.

6.   Alson sold an additional 448,340 shares of TOL in the second quarter of 2005. Both sales were prior to the Wall Street Journal article. Both sales amounted to 64.2% of Alson's holdings in TOL.

The bottom line? Alson was dumping a large holding of TOL while discounting the housing bubble, and Barasky failed to disclose that fact while putting his money where his mouth was. Money managers implore their investors to keep their money invested while they follow a different direction with their own capital.

A notable incident happened in Phoenix at about the same time. A local entrepreneur owned one of the largest and most successful residential real estate brokerage firms in Arizona. He was considered, and rightly so, to be an expert in the business. When interviewed by the Arizona Republic he adamantly declared, "There is no real estate bubble." No problem there. Everyone is entitled to an opinion, and obviously this gentleman had an informed opinion. However, within a few months of this pronouncement, the entrepreneur sold his firm which would turn out to be at the top of the market. Was the buyer, whose sales volume has appreciably shrunk in 2007, influenced by the public representations of the seller? I've always admired owners who sell at a market top. I can't understand why buyers can't arrive at the same conclusion.

On a more grandiose scale was the sale of Golden West Financial to Wachovia Corp. in the fall of 2006 at the absolute top of the market. Herb and Marian Sandler ran the mom-and-pop thrift for an amazing 39 years through all those boom and bust cycles elicited earlier. The sales price? $24 billion.

The vast majority of Golden West's loans were option ARMs primarily to California residents. It isn't surprising that Wachovia's non-performing loans jumped 19% in the second quarter of 2007. About 60% of that increase was attributable to the "legacy" from Golden West. If you were a shareholder of Wachovia and have seen your stock drop over 20% since the acquisition, you might question management's perspective. Hats off, though, to mom and pop Sandler.

Remaining in Phoenix, which was regarded as one of the hottest residential markets in the country, bothersome new stories were popping up amongst the cacti. (Occasionally our delivery person impales our newspaper on a cactus.) An article written by Catherine Reagor of the Arizona Republic on 6-09-05 was entitled "Interest -Only Loans Soar." In 2000, she reported, only one out of ten home loans in Arizona were interest-only or potentially high-risk mortgages. By the first quarter of 2005 one in three loans in Arizona were interest only, which was second in the country only to the District of Columbia. Interest-only loans were most prevalent in areas like Phoenix, where prices were rising rapidly.

Reagor explained, "Many homeowners and most real estate investors aren't concerned about making any principal payments, because they plan on flipping the house for a profit long before the interest-only part of their loan expires." These borrowers never envisioned, of course, that the music would stop when they were in possession of the house. When I was a kid, the last one with a chair when the music stopped was the big winner. Now, the last one left with the house is the wiener.

In this same article two industry mavens were also quoted who again have to be remanded for their incredulity.

"I used to think that interest-only loans were sort of a stupid move but I have changed my mind since historically the Valley's homes always appreciate." —Jay Butler, Director of the Arizona Real Estate Center at ASU.

"Buyers using interest-only loans should be ok because the worst

housing appreciation we will ever see in Phoenix will probably be *percent per year."*—Greg Swann, a real estate agent with Phoenix-u Bloodhound Home Marketing Group.

To Jay, who certainly knows that there were times like 1974, 1980, and 1990/1992 when Valley homes depreciated, his first inclination was correct. To Gregg, who was caught up in the mania, I suggest that he send their bloodhound out to see if he can sniff out a home that will appreciate 6 to 9% this year.

Agents were engulfed by the forest but couldn't see the trees or hear them bark.

In May of 2005 Fed Chairman Alan Greenspan gave a speech at the New York Economic Club. He answered questions regarding how long the steep housing price gains seen in many parts of the nation could go on.

"It's pretty clear that it's an unsustainable underlying pattern,"[9] the Chairman said in perhaps what was, in his vernacular, one of his least oblique statements. *"People are reaching to be able to pay the prices to be able to move into a home,"* he added. And lo and behold, he mentioned the "B" word. *"...it's hard not see that there are a lot of local bubbles."*

So, given what highly regarded economists like Shiller had ascertained and opined and what the head of our central bank knew and publicly disclosed, what were the MOD doing to presumably cool an overheated market? Surprise, surprise! They were, incredibly, adding fuel to the fire.

A headline in the July 26, 2005, Wall Street Journal caught my unbelieving eye: ***Mortgage Lenders Loosen Standards.***

According to Ruth Simon, the journalist for the Wall Street Journal, here is what some of the big guns in the home lending business were doing:[10]

"In a recent move, Chase Home Finance, a unit of J.P. Morgan Chase & Co., this spring began allowing some of its customers to take out home equity loans without having their incomes verified... Loans with little

ntation have grown in popularity industry wide."

ywide Financial Corp ... recently cut by 20 points the core borrowers with bigger loan amounts need to qualify ore popular loan programs."

With the handwriting on the wall but for those too blind to see, what was the reason given by the banks and mortgage lenders to loosen standards?

"We're just offering the product that a lot of our competitors have offered," says U.S. Bank President Dan Arrigoni. *"If anything, we have to think about loosening them if we want to compete."*

You may be acquainted with the herd mentality of sheep. A herd will follow the leader (the one with a bell around its neck) over a cliff, if that's what path the leader chooses. In a snowstorm, the vulnerable creatures will huddle so close together that many of them will suffocate. That's what the banks and savings and loans did in the 80s that led to 747 institutions falling off a cliff in 1990. But there was a different twist this time: Bankers and mortgage lenders, unlike their woolly counterparts, have the ability to recall those dire days of the RTC. This time was different, they surmised. They <u>sold</u> the loans they originated. If the real estate market crashed (and we now know it did), they would suffer no loss, no recourse. Neat, huh? Briefly, here's how securitization of subprime debt worked as so capably described by Jonathan R. Laing in Barron's:

"How did the U.S. subprime-loan market morph into a ticking time bomb? The answer begins, and ends, with Wall Street's ingenuity, which was enhanced by something curiously close to alchemy. To raise the aforementioned trillion dollars to purchase the flood of new subprime mortgages from lenders, brokerage firms invented residential-mortgage-backed securities, or MBS, which they sold to institutional investors. These securities consisted of different slices, or

tranches, of bonds, with triple-A and other highly rated tranches having repayment priority as the original borrowers paid back principal and interest.

Investors at the lower reaches of the waterfall -- that is, the triple-B and triple-B-minus tranches -- earned much higher interest rates on their debt to compensate for the considerably greater risks residing in these securities. If the mortgage pool underlying an MBS were to suffer a principal loss of just 7% from defaults and foreclosures, some MBS experts calculate, these tranches would be cut off from the pool's capital flows and rendered worthless.

To facilitate the sale of the higher-risk tranches, and arguably gin up more fees, Wall Street repackaged many triple-B mortgage-backed securities, and even more of the triple-B-minus tranches, into new securities called mezzanine collateralized debt obligations, or CDOs, which also were sold to institutional investors. "Mezzanine" referred to the difficult-to-sell securities that sat in the middle of the MBS capital structure, between the higher-rated securities at the top and the high-yielding, equity-like tranches at the bottom. The latter were much-coveted by speculators.

It is at the mezzanine level that the so-called alchemy occurred, when bond-rating agencies such as Moody's and Standard & Poor's rated some 80% of the principal amount of the triple-B tranches as triple-A. Under the "grade inflation" that came to be accepted in subprime-CDO land, the top 60% of the mezzanine capital structure was called "super-senior" triple-A.

As one dealer in MBS told Barron's, "Mezzanine subprime CDOs are all the same junk." But because one slice of the CDOs was subordinated to the rest, the rating agencies allowed most of these highly speculative securities "to be turned into gold."[11]

Laing's bottom-line piece appeared July 9, 2007. In 2005 virtually no one outside the MOD knew how the new system worked—nor did they care.

Fixed income securities, namely bonds, are rated by various companies such as Standard & Poors (S&P), Moody's Investor's Service, and others that use more than 20 grades to describe how likely a bond is to default. The higher the grade, the safer the bond. U.S. Treasury bonds are the safest, which S&P rates at AAA or top investment grade. Speculative grade or "junk bonds" like the country of Ecuador are rated CCC by S&P. Prospective buyers of bonds (or, for purposes of our discussion, mortgage bonds) depended almost entirely on the bond's rating to make a decision whether or not to buy the debt of the issuer. Now that the Wall Street firms had packaged the subprime loans into CDOs, the questions remained: how could they peddle this junk to investors? The ingenuity of Wall Street found a way to put lipstick on a pig and pass that baby off as an investment grade bond. No one other than a limited few inside this arcane corner of the mortgage market knew what was going on, but turning junk into gold was the alchemy that made subprime loans grow to a massive market of over $1 *trillion* in just five years!

How could that possibly happen? These rating agencies have been around forever and as are unimpeachable as (some) men of cloth.

In 2000, S&P made a decision that would come back—like Marley's ghost— to haunt them. They concluded that a mortgage that involves a "piggyback" where the borrower simultaneously takes out a second loan for the down payment was no more likely to default than a standard mortgage. Somehow that decision morphed into subprime mortgages, and we now have a translucent insight as to why it occurred.

Wall Street firms who underwrote the CDOs worked with the rating companies to make certain that the bond had high enough ratings to be marketable. The subprime market became extremely lucrative for the rating companies as their fees became double what they would receive for rating corporate bonds. Moody's Investor's Service took in around $3 billion in fees from 2002 to 2006 for rating securities built from loans and other debt pools including the CDOs. Wall Street and mortgage companies "shopped" for ratings.

The rating firms deny that they were guilty of "bargaining" for ratings, but some critics such as Ohio Attorney General Marc Dann contend that the rating firms "had so much to gain from issuing investment grade ratings that they had 'symbiotic relationship' with the banks and mortgage companies."[12]

By the second half of 2006 Moody's observed that a large number of subprime borrowers weren't even making their _first_ payments. By July 2006 over 33% of the loans in Washington Mutual's subprime pool were delinquent or in foreclosure. Belatedly, late in 2006 Moody's and S&P slashed their ratings. S&P downgraded some loans from A- to below investment grade BB or "junk." That's when the 'fit hit the shan.'

If you're not scratching your head, rolling your eyes, or mad as hell by now, I'm like Cool Hand Luke who has had "a failure to communicate." Let's review what happened here.

1.   In 2002 President Bush had an altruistic goal to provide home ownership to low-income Americans. Congress, despite historical evidence that such a program would again be costly to taxpayers and detrimental to those it purported to benefit, passes the American Down Payment Dream Act.

2.   In 2001 and 2002 the Federal Reserve Board and the Federal Open Market Committee promulgate a strategy of cheap, easy credit to boost consumer spending that further indentured millions of Americans and fueled a real estate bubble that put the entire economy at risk.

3.   During this five-year period neither the Fed, government agencies, mortgage bankers, nor bond rating companies took any action to control or prevent the excesses and abuse that have created unstable market conditions.

4.   The five-year market mania created short term income and capital gains for investors, speculators, real estate professionals, mortgage lenders, title companies, home builders, developers, appraisers, etc., and promoted dramatic increase in consumer spending without real economic growth.

5.   Investment banking firms on Wall Street racked up

outrageous profits packaging, underwriting, and selling CDOs. Principals and employees of the top four firms pocketed $36 billion in bonuses alone in 2006 from CDOs and other products (Chapter Six) in addition to enjoying the highest earnings of any industry in the U.S.

So, what is the point of this exercise?

THE RICH GOT RICHER AND THE MIDDLE CLASS GOT POORER

A cynic might respond 'So what is startling about this revelation? Hasn't that always been the case?"

No, this time it was different.

In the past Wall Street scams that have not been discussed here—the 300% write-off oil and gas and equipment partnerships of the 70s, the junk bonds of the 80s, the .com bubble of the 90s—all of them have one common denominator. Wall Street created products for their brokers to market to affluent prospects. The investors who bought these products had capital to invest. They were, at a minimum, "middle" middle class. They were not the working middle class who had little savings or inclination to invest or speculate.

Here's why it is different this time. Wall Street was able to create enormous profits and fees from a class of people who had little or no money: the *lower* middle class.

In most cases, the homeowners leveraged the only asset they had—their home. In addition, most of them who received "cash out" from the refinance didn't invest the money ... they spent it. It's gone, and in most cases it can't ever be replaced. Wall Street (probably unknowingly at first) found an untapped market, much like discovering oil in Appalachia. These Wall Street MOD exploited this class of Americans without any concern for their lives by appealing to their most vulnerable weakness—*Greed*.

Predatory lenders, such as New Century Financial (NEW— noted below) deliberately and aggressively preyed upon low-income and middle-class Americans to market their loans. In January 2007 NEW originated an incredible $4.2 billion in debt, all subprime, and the large percentage were "no doc" (document) loans, just one month before they filed for bankruptcy!

In short, the applicants were not required to document their sources of income. In most cases the applicant may not have had sufficient income to make interest payments and used, for a short period of time, principal from the loan to make payments.

Many loans, I suspect (and investigation will ultimately reveal), were fraudulent, and the applicant took the money and ran with no intent of making any payments. A large percentage, however, were made to folk who must have been blinded by the prospect of having a wad of cash in their hands for the first time in their lives—and they spent it. A $50,000 loan to a 75-year-old widow living on Social Security who lost the home where she had lived for 30 years would be unconscionable. But to the mortgage broker, it was a quick, easy sale with a nice commission. Here are a few actual local cases:

A Scottsdale couple in their mid-60s borrowed $1,000,000 on their home using a Pay Option ARM loan that had an initial start rate of 1%, tied to LIBOR. Their home appraised for $1,200,000. The couple signed a statement verifying their assets and income but provided no documents. They maintain that they did not understand that they had negative amortization and that the principal amount of the loan would increase each month. As the monthly payment increased, they attempted to refinance. Due to a lower appraisal, prepayment penalties, and accrued principal due to the negative amortization, the couple discovered that they were several hundred thousand dollars "underwater" on their mortgage. Chances are, they will lose their home.

In another case, a California resident contracted to buy a four-plex in Phoenix. He represented to the lender that he would live in one of the units but never did. He obtained a 90% interest only "no doc" loan. As the demand for this type of residential property began to decline and the buyer could not flip the property as intended, he managed to refinance the four-plex, cash out most of his down payment, and walked from the obligation. The property sold at auction.

A 70-year-old man bought a primary residence in a popular resort area in Northern Arizona. In March 2007 his prospective home appraised for $1,170,000. He borrowed the maximum amount available on a Pay Option ARM. Within a few months, as his monthly payment increased, he attempted to refinance to a fixed rate mortgage. An appraisal only six months after the original loan was funded came in at $700,000. This story begs the obvious question: who was the appraiser, and was there collusion with the owner or any other party?

In order to fully understand and appreciate the gravity of the subprime "mess" you need to learn about the travails of Roger Rodriquez, a truck driver from Colorado.[13]

Lured by internet and radio adds promoting easy loan approval, Roger called a company by the name of Equity-Relief.com whose slogan was "Debt Relief is stress relief at Equity-Relief.com." Within weeks in 2004 Roger had secured an $88,000 loan through this broker with CIT Group, a large financial conglomerate. His ARM had an initial monthly payment of $545 with an introductory rate of 6.3%. In two years, however, the rate would reset up to a maximum of 12.3%.

Within five months CIT had sold Roger's loan to RBS Greenwich Capital, a unit of the Royal Bank of Scotland. In February 2005, RBS packaged Roger's loan along with 4,853 others and sold them to a trust called Soundview 2005-1. RBS sold a total of $778 million in notes to this trust. Each time the purchase and sale of Roger's note passed through the hands of these firms a fee or profit was earned, but none of the institutions would indicate any amounts.

One buyer of the Soundview 2005-1 notes was a Mr. Kelsoe, a senior portfolio manager of Morgan Keegan & Co., a Memphis, Tennessee investment firm. At the end of 2005 Mr. Kelsoe's fund (RMK Select High Income Fund) showed a five-year average annual gain of 14%, and the fund was rated the best of its class in the U.S., which brought Mr. Kelsoe huge celebrity and capital.

By February 2006 Roger's fortunes, as well as those of the RMK fund, turned south. Due to an accident Roger lost his job, and his income decreased while his mortgage payment reset to $700 per month. Unable to make his payment, Roger and his wife filed for bankruptcy and ultimately lost their home.

By the end of June 2005 Soundview reported that four out of ten loans were at least 30 days in arrears, and by August Mr. Kelsoe's Select High Income Fund posted a loss of 28% for the month —ranking his fund dead last amongst his peer group. Mr. Kelsoe, in a letter to his shareholders, said, "the ocean of liquidity has quickly become a desert." A lawyer who had invested in one of Kelsoe's funds accused the fund manager of "hiding under his desk" and said he "should have the fortitude to face the public and explain ... what he intended to do."

This tale has ended badly for everyone who has touched Roger's mortgage. CIT plans to shut down its mortgage business and lay off 550 employees. RBS Greenwich has laid off 44 employees, and 1,760 jobs are in limbo. Kelsoe and his broker-dealer will undoubtedly face a barrage of investor lawsuits which could bring them close to the brink of bankruptcy. For Roger, who now lives in a low-income apartment in Denver, depression has reached the point where his wife fears that her husband is suicidal.

Just imagine, there could be millions of individual tragedies just like Roger's, but it's those at the bottom of the scale that lose the most. The subprime mess could be the greatest case of financial inequity in American history. *Greed* created bad judgement as well as outright fraud in all stages up and down the real estate food chain.

The Arizona Department of Financial Institutions (DFI) is the governing body for all financial lenders in the state which has its counterparts nationwide. In June 2007 Arizona passed a law making residential mortgage fraud a class 2 or 4 felony. Prior to its enactment, DFI fined First Financial Title Agency of Arizona $20,000 and its President $10,000 for not supervising one of its escrow officers who conducted a fraudulent loan transaction on behalf of two real estate agents.

Back to 2005. Where were the banking regulators during this period? Ms. Simon reported:

"In May (2005), in response to concerns about looser underwriting standards bank regulators issued their first ever guidelines for credit-risk management for home equity lending. Regulators are working on new guidelines for mortgage lenders."

If guidelines were handed down from the Office of the Comptroller of the Currency and other agencies around this period, it appears that they had little or no impact on loosened lending practices. The beat went on. Profits at commercial banks from loan originations were almost outrageous—and with the ability to borrow from the Fed at 1% and no recourse to the loan they originated, why should they be deterred? Cheap, easy credit and a virtually inexhaustible supply of money added more fuel to a fire of **Greed** absorbing the nation. Loan losses, however were shifted to another department of the bank, as we'll soon learn.

What was the mind set at the Fed? A small excerpt from the September 20, 2005, FOMC meeting is incomprehensible:

"...consumption would probably expand at a moderate pace—perhaps a little below the pace of income growth once the increase in house prices slowed to more historical typical rates."

There are two major flaws in the FOMC's thinking as reflected in these minutes. Consumption had now become 70% of the GDP vs. the norm of 66%, and consumer spending was well in excess of income growth ... fueled, of course, by cash-out refinancing. The Fed's belief (at least that memorialized in the minutes for public consumption) that house prices would moderate to historical norm was delusional. How do you stop a freight train going downhill without brakes?

The Fed could have put the brakes on the subprime market if it desired to do so. Under a law called the Home Ownership & Equity Protection Act, the Fed had the power to prohibit "acts or practices in connection with mortgage loans that the board finds to be unfair, deceptive, or associated with abusive lending practices, or that are otherwise not in the interest of the borrowers." Now, of course, after the predatory MOD have cleaned out the hen house, the politicians and regulators are mobilizing their muscle to punish the miscreants. How much cash will they recover for the babes in ARMS? A minuscule amount ... but that's only an estimate.

Was the FOMC holding their meeting on another planet? The evidence was overwhelming that the residential real estate market was at manic levels and everyone (particularly the old folks on the FOMC) knew all manic markets end badly. So why didn't the Fed's act? For what it's worth—and I hope it's worth the price of this book—you've got my unbiased opinion. *Greed*!

The money center and commercial banks were making so much money they must have implored the Fed to refrain from applying the brakes. Contrary to well-established mythology, the banking industry, Wall Street, and key politicos call the shots—until, of course, everything goes to hell in a handbasket; then the Fed emerges above the mess to re-establish its 'independence' as it now is doing.

I know this is a hard to swallow as a Move Free tablet, but when you tear down the curtain of mystique the answer is as clear as the San Francisco Bay Bridge on a semi-foggy day. We're all munchkins in the land of OZ. Dorothy discovered that the all-powerful wizard was nothing but a meek, mealy-mouthed mortal hiding behind an imposing facade. Never before in recent U.S. economic history have so many informed experts recently questioned the role of the Federal Reserve in this squalid affair. Stay tuned as we also hear from the "maestro" himself, Alan Greenspan.

Since there was little or no oversight or direction to the banking industry, you've probably got a pretty good idea what was happening in the unregulated arena, where the ever-growing predatory MOD played the game with no rules other than make as many points on loans as possible before an umpire blew a whistle. The story of New Century Financial (NEW) wins the flagrant foul award hands down.

The story of New Century Financial (NEW) is either one of an American dream dissolving into a nightmare or a well-calculated scam orchestrated by its founders.

NEW was organized by CEO Brad Morrice and two other officers at Option One Mortgage in 1995 in Irvine, California, and operated as a traditional mortgage company for almost ten years prior to converting to a

Real Estate Investment Trust (REIT). When NEW went public via an initial public offering (IPO), Morrice and the other key executives "cashed out," piggybacking their personal stock holdings in the IPO. At that point NEW focused its marketing plan almost exclusively on subprime lending.

Morrice and four other key executives promptly set each of their salaries at $2,282,727 per year plus liberal perks including stock options. NEW was a high-profile flyer in the mortgage business using well-known TV personality Bob Vila as their spokesman through their Home 123 division. The company also entered into a sponsoring deal with NASCAR and helped sponsor the Chip Ganassi Racing with Felix Sabates Team, occasionally appearing on the #42 race car driven by Jaime McMurray. As of January 1, 2007, NEW had approximately 7,200 full-time employees, had a market capitalization of $1.75 billion, and was listed on the NYSE. By March 2007, however, this NASCAR sponsor crashed and burned when it received $150 million in margin calls from its warehouse lenders and ceased operations.

More than 100 mortgage companies closed their doors in 2007, so why is NEW's failure a big deal?

One, NEW was, by March 2007, the second largest subprime lender in the U.S.

Two, but more importantly, is how Morrice and his key executives profited handsomely from a business plan that was doomed to fail from the onset.

These principals of NEW, seasoned veterans of the mortgage business, knew (or should have known) that a mortgage portfolio consisting of borrowers with a proven record of defaulting on their obligations would, within a few years, implode. Point is, did they really care?

After "cashing out" at the IPO, granting themselves generous salaries and bonuses, and securing millions of dollars in profits from exercised stock options, why should the principals be concerned abut the ongoing status of NEW? Why should they be concerned about the human debris left in the path of NEW's tornadic marketing plan? Ultimately, federal FBI, and state investigation may reveal that NEW was indeed a scam, and Morrice and his cohorts may have to spend a goodly portion of their bounty feeding the sharks to defend themselves.

Chapter Six
Goldilocks & Superman
(The Story of Goldilocks & The 3 Bears)

Lawrence Kudlow is in love with Goldilocks. Larry is the host of CNBC's Kudlow and Company, which is a one-hour show that appears Monday through Friday. Larry didn't create "Goldi," but he promotes her tirelessly as a metaphor for a perfect economy that's "not too hot, not too cold, but 'just right'." You remember this fable:

"Once upon a time, there was a little girl named Goldilocks. She went for a walk in the forest, Pretty soon, she came upon a house. She knocked and, when no one answered, she walked right in.

At the table in the kitchen, there were three bowls of porridge. Goldilocks was hungry. She tasted the porridge from the first bowl.

"This porridge is too hot!" she exclaimed.

So, she tasted the porridge from the second bowl.

"This porridge is too cold," she said.

So, she tasted the last bowl of porridge.

"Ahhh, this porridge is just right," she said happily and she ate it all up.

You remember the rest of the story so...

Here is an excerpt from Larry's show on Friday, October 5, 2007, that exploits the fable of the sweet young lady who brazenly visits the home of the three bears:

Recession Off the Table

*Today's solid jobs report gain of 110,000 for September, and an 118,000 upward revision to the prior two months blows recession off the table. Particularly encouraging is the 463,000 gain in household employment. It sets up a Goldilocks stock market rally that could add another 1,000 points to the Dow over the next six months. (*Wrong!

Emphasis added.*)*

Fed bigwig Donald Kohn strongly hinted a dollar protection program that rules out additional Fed rate cuts for the time being. I agree with Kohn. The Fed's shock and awe 50 basis point rate cut in September has caused a loosening in the credit market freeze-up and provided a liquidity cushion for the entire economy. The Fed has done its job. (Wrong Again! Emphasis added.*)*

With inflation indexes running about 2 percent, domestic price stability is on course. Housing woes will take a percent off GDP for the next several quarters, leaving about 2 percent growth and 2 percent inflation. It is the quintessential Goldilocks soft landing scenario. (Two wrongs don't make a right! Emphasis added.)

Kudlow, who served as an economic advisor to Ronald Reagan during his Presidency, "aims to be right on business, right on America, and right on the money." He's an unapologetic cheerleader for Wall Street, free enterprise, and Republicanism. Nothing wrong with that—if you happen to be a Republican ... but he is guilty, as are almost all of his CNBC cohorts, of constantly parroting the "no inflation" line as evidence that "Goldi" is alive and well. Larry will go to any length of logic to establish that there is not, and there will not be, any inflation in the U.S.—unless the Democrats control the Presidency *and* both houses of Congress (which is partisan nonsense). He was dead wrong in his economic assessment as of October 5, 2007.

Not all Wall Street movers and shakers, however, are in love with "Goldi." Art Cashin, a floor trader who has been on Wall Street for at least five decades and to whom I can equate, was asked by CNBC's Mark Haines after a particularly bad day in the market:

"Hey Art? What the heck happened to Goldilocks?"

"The problem is that Goldilocks is running around with Britney and Lindsay," the old pro replied.

While Wall Street and its clients benefit from "Goldi's" image, average middle-class America, particularly seniors receiving Social Security who have little or no capital invested in equities, receive only a 2%

to 3% raise in their benefits each year. But, their true cost of living is considerably greater than that. There are currently 47.7 million people receiving Social Security benefits according to the national Jobs for All Coalition ... thirty million are retirees who receive an average of $955 per month in benefits. It's fair to assume that on a minimum basis, for possibly 50% of the nearly 50 million people, this payment is what they live on. The wealthy greatly benefit from "Goldi's" deception, but a great multitude of Americans are deprived by it. Another example why the rich get richer and the poor get poorer. The nation is ripe for a "No Senior Left Behind" movement.

I will offer Kudlow's "Flip Flop" message from the same program in support of my position that the Fed takes its "direction" from the rich and powerful. To wit:

A Heckuva Good Flip-Flop

In politics—especially on the campaign trail -- key issue flip-flops are usually quite damaging. That's not necessarily the case in monetary policy. Fed head Ben Bernanke had a whopper of a flip-flop nearly two months ago. But it was a very positive flip-flop for financial markets, the economy, and maybe even the sinking fortunes of the Republican Party.

Earlier this week, Wharton school finance lecturer Ken Thomas shed some light on the Fed chair's flip-flop. Using the Freedom of Information Act, Thomas was able to unearth Bernanke's calendar of phone calls and meetings during the height of this summer's credit seize-up. By piecing together a logical narrative, he discovered that a day after the Fed's August 7th decision to keep rates steady, and maintain their focus on inflation worries, Mr. Bernanke received a phone call from Wall Street powerhouse and former Clinton Treasury Secretary, Citigroup's **Robert Rubin (emphasis added).**

Markets were already in disarray from the credit seize-up that started in mid-July. And while Thomas does not know the actual content of the Rubin call, subsequent calls and events strongly suggest that Bernanke rapidly changed his mind and steered the Fed towards a series of massive money additions to the banking system and a half point discount rate cut.

All of which led to a shock and awe, liquidity-adding 50 basis point drop in the Fed funds rate on September 18th.

According to the Bernanke logs, the 5 pm Rubin call on August 8th was followed by a 7:30 am next day breakfast with Bush Treasury man Henry Paulson, and an 11 am meeting with legendary mortgage expert Lou Ranieri. (Ranieri pioneered mortgage backed securitizations, the very bonds that were collapsing as a result of the subprime mortgage virus that had already begun infecting the financial system.)

At 2:00 pm later that same day, the Fed chair also met with Ray Dalio, head of Bridgewater, the 4th largest U.S. hedge fund, as well as other hedge fund magnates. At 4:30 pm, Mr. Bernanke was on a conference call with his fellow FOMC members, undoubtedly to discuss a 180-degree Fed change of heart.

In fact, over the next few weeks, Bernanke participated in no fewer than thirty-five separate conference calls with fellow Fed operatives -- a complete departure from the chairman's earlier style of not having conference calls.

As we know now, the Fed started pouring in new liquidity Friday August 10th with a major announcement. On August 17th they slashed their base discount rate for member bank loans by 50 basis points, and of course a month later, slashed their overnight target rate.

As Mr. Thomas notes, no one can be sure if this narrative is correct, simply because there is no available record of what was actually said during these calls and meetings. But it seems pretty clear that Robert Rubin started a chain reaction with his callback on August 8th. This was only one day after the Fed's hold-the line policy decision that so disappointed financial markets and intensified the credit turmoil that many people feared would spillover into the economy and lead to recession.

Essentially, the academic Mr. Bernanke became a hands-on market participant through his contacts with Rubin, Paulson, the hedgies, and others. His learning curve efforts to reach out to savvy financial market players put him in touch with the real world. Basically, Bernanke embarked on a 5-week journey that shook world credit markets out of their financial *panic and started the healing process that continues to progress right up to this very day.*

Most folks would agree that while far from being completely solved, the credit crunch is easing. And of course, the stock markets have rebounded dramatically with the Dow hovering near its all-time 14,000 high. Stock markets all around the world have recovered. And the outlook for economic growth, though still uncertain, is nonetheless much brighter than it was back on August 7th when the Fed first turned its back on the emerging credit crisis.

Without question, Bernanke made a mistake in early August. But this is a case where his flip-flop was a very positive move, one that enhanced his credibility in U.S. and world markets.

The Fed's "independence" is a myth promulgated over the years that communicates to the public that this body of economic and banking genius acts in the best interest of the country as a whole. What do you think?

Author's Note: Kudlow's pronouncement that "It is the quintessential Goldilocks soft landing scenario." And "The Fed has done its job" was quite premature. The credit crisis was far from over when Kudlow made this proclamation as CDO losses at Merrill Lynch and Citigroup continued to panic the markets and the Fed continued to lower rates and inject billions into the system. Kudlow is "singing" to the choir of CNBC advertisers whose goal is to use the massive market exposure to attract and retain the viewer's investment capital.

After WWII, there was a popular slogan:

WHAT IS GOOD FOR GENERAL MOTORS IS GOOD FOR THE COUNTRY

A dramatic shift occurred in the ensuing 40 years that reversed this mantra. High wages and benefits, poor product, a strong dollar policy, and the political will to promote globalization changed not only the auto industry but virtually all manufacturing in the U.S. We've now reached the:

WHAT IS GOOD FOR WALL STREET IS GOOD FOR THE COUNTRY

As most know, artificial insemination, or AI, is a fertilization procedure in which sperm is artificially placed into a woman's cervix or uterus, and if the procedure is successful the woman conceives. It's also a procedure that makes the male only partially relevant. Maybe irrelevant in some cases.

What on God's green earth does "AI" have to do with **Greed**? Placing myself at risk for being too clever as I attempt to add color to this story, I can't resist the temptation to create a modern fable. Let's call it "GOLDILOCKS & SUPERMAN."

Once upon a time not long ago in a land called UZ lived a girl by the name of GOLDILOCKS. "Goldi," as a creation and metaphor for the economy, enjoyed immense popularity because her disposition was neither too hot nor too cold, but just right. Her fame and reputation soared even higher after her escape from the den of the three bears. Despite the admiration and respect she commanded, however, "Goldi" knew there was a void in her life. She wanted a mate.

The Wall Street Investment Bankers who nurtured "Goldi" keenly wanted her to marry and, more importantly, have a family. The Bankers introduced "Goldi" to Superman who, metaphorically, represented manufacturing in the land of UZ.

Superman was older and was losing his strength and stature in the nation, but the Bankers hoped that "Goldi" could revitalize the former hero of UZ and again bring glory to the worn-out industry.

The wedding was a huge success, and the marriage had a positive impact on all the markets. The land of UZ anxiously awaited an announcement that "Goldi" was expecting. Time went by, but there was no word. Unfortunately, Superman was impotent. (Now you know where we're headed.)

The Bankers suggested that "Goldi" have "AI" from an undisclosed outside source. Nine months after the fertilization took place "Goldi" gave birth to TRIPLETS! The three were named:

Private Equity
Leveraged Buyout
Stock Buy-Back

The Investment Bankers and Wall Street were ecstatic.

Over the years "Goldi" and Superman's family grew by virtue of continued artificial insemination. And no one in the land of UZ (except the Bankers) knew how this miracle occurred, but the rich and powerful profited handsomely.

Here's the rest of the story.

During the summer of 2007, just as the subprime news was filtering down to an unknowing public, *Greed* began to turn to FEAR amongst the populace. The Dow Jones Industrial Average (DJIA) reached an all-time high of 14,000. Traditionally markets climb a "wall of worry," but there was something different this time. The markets were being stimulated artificially—thus the tie-in with my little fable.

Stock buy-backs are companies buying back their own stock. In the Old Economy public companies would often buy back their own stock because they determined that it was under-valued. Possibly their stock decreased in price due to a non-recurring earnings problem, or a strike by union workers, or rumors that ultimately would be proven to be untrue. The company would purchase the stock for cash on the open market and hold for appreciation.

But this is the New Economy.

In the first quarter of 2007, S&P-500 companies spent $117.7 billion buying back their own shares. In the second quarter Home Depot, Inc. announced that it would buy back $22.5 billion of its stock; Wal-Mart, $15 billion; and GE, $8 billion. All these companies are part of the DJIA. Federal Reserve figures show that non-financial companies took $128 billion of stock off the market through buy-backs in the first quarter, while at the same time they took on $130 billion in debt. "Companies don't appear to be using their new borrowings to finance new plants or equipment," says Northern Trust economist Paul Kasriel. " The data support the view that corporations are stepping up their credit borrowings to finance their share buy-backs," he says.

Why would these companies do this at a market top?

1.	Stock buy-backs reduce the number of shares outstanding, and in most cases the share price will increase. Buy-backs did supercharge a rally in 2007 as this supply of shares decreased.

2.	Buy-backs can benefit corporate executives with large holdings of unexercised stock options. They could exercise the options and immediately sell the stock for a profit or hold the stock, since it would represent a larger stake in the company.

3.	Buy-backs can also benefit corporate executives whose compensation may be tied to, in part, earnings and share price targets.

4.	Investors prefer buy-backs (if they hold the stock) rather than dividends because the dividends are taxable.

S&P reports as of the third quarter 2007, $1.8 trillion in stock buy-backs is sitting in the treasuries of S&P 500 companies. Buy-backs boosted the prices of these stocks on the upside.[14] What happens if and when these companies decide to liquidate these shares? The pros will win and most of the amateurs will lose.

Writers occasionally are able to achieve recognition (albeit for themselves only) for their foresight. Such is the case for my above position regarding the buy-backs. The following incident was learned after the buy-back piece above was written.

The New England Teamsters and Trucking Industry Pension Fund[15] has filed an action accusing the CEO of Countrywide Financial Corp, Angelo Mozilo, of artificially inflating the Countrywide stock for the benefit of Mozilo and key executives. Specifically, it accused the officials of the company of improperly using $2 billion in cash to repurchase the stock. The suit alleges that that purchase enabled the executives to sell $842 million of Countrywide shares at artificially high prices at the expense of shareholders. So, AI was for real.

Ironically and supportive to the suit, Countrywide (which possesses a huge subprime portfolio) faced a severe liquidity crunch when the meltdown occurred and had to get an emergency infusion of cash from Bank of America equal to the amount the company used to buy the stock. (The Federal Home Loan Bank of Atlanta lent Countrywide $51 billion to keep its doors open. And recently, Bank of America acquired Countrywide and all of its contingent liabilities.)

Stock buy-backs are an example of Goldilock's illusion of a "just right" economy. Little real growth drove these prices higher. The market was artificially inseminated! How big a role did *Greed* play in this niche of the money game? Significant, but that's only an estimate.

U.S. investors cheered when the DJIA and the S&P 500 reached new highs, but the dollar's decline was devastating for foreign buyers of our assets. To them "Goldi" had lost as much in value as Britney had in fans. According to Macro Mavens, a Wall Street research firm, investors from the following countries saw the S&P-500 index decline since the March 2000 peak to May 2007:

37% in Euros
37% in Norwegian Kroner
36% in Canadian Dollars
24% in British Pounds
9% in Russian Rubles

And, despite the decline in the U.S. dollar, the May 2007 trade deficit was $64 billion. How much longer will foreign investors continue to support "Goldi's" fable?

The Goldilocks economy spawned a plethora of Private-Equity (P-E) deals that also super charged the equity markets. P-E are companies that are not publically held and, for the purposes of this discussion, are involved in the acquisition of those companies that are listed on exchanges and are taken private. P-Es could be firms that specialize in buy-outs, hedge funds that are seeking higher risk-reward opportunities, investment bankers, or any number of a multitude of players who seized upon the global *Greed* pandemic fueled by a virtually unlimited pool of liquidity. Here are a few: (Wall Street Journal, 8-01-07)

Private Equity	Company Purchased	Amount
Apollo Management, LP	Linens N' Things, Inc.	$1.3 Billion
Avista Capital Partners	Star Tribune	$530 Million
	Freescale Semi-Holdings	$17.6 Billion
Apollo Management, LP	Realogy Corp	$6.7 Billion

The companies listed above have one thing in common. All of them have performed well *below* expectations not long after the ink had dried on the purchases.

The Star Tribune, acquired in March, 2007, is operating 20% below its cash flow projections. Linen 'N Things, which was purchased by Apollo in February 2006, has had a cash flow of $130 million less than projected for its 2006 fiscal year and the sale of its bonds to purchase the company are off 15% since February.

Apollo could not have purchased Realogy, a national residential real estate broker, at a worse time. Sales have plummeted since the company was taken private in April 2007, which should not be a surprise to anyone but the P-E, and the yields on its bonds have climbed to 13.1%.

Author's Note: Andrew Bary in the December 3, 2007 issue of Barron's FN validated the decline of the LBOs mentioned above. Realogy's cash flow in 2007 will just barely meet its debt service and 2008 could be worse. Some of its subordinated notes are presently selling at 38% discount. Linen 'N Things is now operating at a substantial loss and its *debt trades at 50% discount. The sponsor, Apollo and its partners, could lose its entire equity investment of $500 million on the deal. 2008 will not be a good year for LBOs unless Goldilocks re-asserts herself as the darling of Wall Street.*

P-E was attracted to cheap credit like moths to a flame, and many of them will suffer a similar demise. In 2005, a then record of $300 billion was loaned to P-E and reached $500 billion last year. Despite the handwriting on the wall, a new record funding will occur in 2007, according to Steven Rattner, Managing Principal at the private investment firm of Quadrangle Group, LLC. Rattner says of the coming credit meltdown, "The current pricing of high-yield bonds will earn an impressive place in the pantheon of investment manias."[16]

Two high-profile names made a deal in July 2007. Blackstone Group, a P-E company that had just gone public, made an offer for Hilton Hotels for $26 billion, while Barron Hilton's granddaughter Paris was doing her worst imitation of a flighty jail bird. This deal brought back recollections to the author, who met with Barron in 1960 and was offered his first job with Hilton as they introduced their credit card, Hilton Carte Blanche. Barron's father, Conrad, had established the hotel chain in San Antonio, New Mexico perhaps 30 years prior, which had to be one of the most humble origins of any hotelier in American history. I know, I've been to the hotel in San Antonio.

The Blackstone Group is one of the big-name players in the leveraged buy-out game (LBO). Their formula had been to take the acquisition target private, load up on debt, leverage the deal to the max, and give their managers a piece of the action so they would work their butts off. Not being captive to short term earnings' objectives, Blackstone created billions of dollars in profit for its employees and investors. So—if the formula worked magic, why change it? Why would Blackstone go public?[17]

There are numerous reasons offered by the company, but the answer is quite simple. Sell out at the top when valuations border on the insane. To wit:

Stephen Swartzman, the Chief Executive of Blackstone Group, LP, received approximately $677 million cash at the initial public offering (IPO) and still held a 24% interest in the new public company, valued at nearly $8 billion. The company made $2.22 billion net income in 2006 as a P-E and Swartzman earned in salary and bonus a total of $77.1 million. Is this pure capitalism at its zenith or its abyss?

There are a couple of observations that should be made here:

1.   There is a massive concentration of wealth on Wall Street that begs the question of inequity when there's a mass majority of an underclass that are losing ground to maintain a reasonable standard of living.

2.   There has been relatively little growth in the U.S. economy over the past six years—about $3.4 trillion in aggregate GDP. What growth that has occurred during this period has been funded by a $6 trillion increase in household debt and a $3 trillion increase in Federal debt, according to Leo Hindery, Jr. writing for Barron's. Not only is this massive accumulation of debt unsustainable, he says, but corporate America "has broken its contract with the middle class."

3.   The Blackstone Group, LP IPO will, in the opinion of this writer, mark the top of this era where *Greed* conquered FEAR and transferred the ultimate pain to middle-class America.

And if that weren't enough, there's the matter of fees.[18]

In an article by Tennile Tracy of the Wall Street Journal, "Private-Equity firms say they are expert at wringing profits out of flagging businesses. It turns out that they are almost twice as good at wringing fees out of their investors." Based in part by a study by two professors at the University of Pennsylvania's Wharton School, the bulk of the P-E firm's earnings comes from "profitably refashioning and reselling the business it buys." The study shows that these firms average about $10 in fees for every $100 they manage, or 10%, compared to $5 out of $100 in carried interest on their cut in the profits when they sell the company.

Assume for the moment that a few of those acquisitions listed above, like Realogy, that are not currently meeting projected earnings, continue to do poorly over the next few years. They become a drag on the P-E's earnings. What do to? Why not take them public again, return the investment to the P-E firm and its investors, make additional fees on the IPO, and dump the dog on the public? Far fetched? If you think so, you haven't got the message.

Based upon this information provided by these unimpeachable sources you could conclude that it's the making of the deal that's the objective and not the merits of the deal. It's the fees, stupid!

One of my close friends who was a broker and a manager for a major Wall Street wire house told me the following story, told to him by a client early in his career:

"Hey man, I got a truck load of sardines for ya—real cheap." Sal said phoning his friend. Mani bought the sardines.

Mani called his buddy Joel, "Joel, I've got a whole truck load of sardines we have to unload real cheap. Are ya' interested?"

Joel bought the sardines and the process continued to several other buyers. A couple days passed and the last buyer called Sal.

"Sal! I just opened one of your cans of sardines and they ain't no good! They're rotten!" he said.

Sal replied, "Hey you old putz—those ain't for eatin', they is for tradin'!"

A perfect example of the Daisy Chain of Derivatives.

When will the investors revolt? When a bunch of deals or trades go bad, and lo and behold, that process has begun. Hedge-funds are the least transparent since P-E guards its numbers.

Hedge-Funds (H-F) are aggressively managed portfolios of investments for sophisticated investors that are advanced investment strategies utilizing leverage, long as well as short, and derivative positions with the goal of generating high returns. Unlike mutual funds, they are unregulated and are pools of money for the wealthy, charging high fees similar to P-Es.

An understanding of the use of leverage is necessary to grasp the impact of what began to unfold in the equity markets in July, 2007.

When you buy a stock and it declines 5% in price, its current asset value is 5% less than you paid for it. If you have a margin account you put up 50% of the cost of the stock, so if the investment loses the same 5%, the current asset value is 10% less than you paid for it. That's the effect of 2:1 leverage, or de-leverage when the value declines.

For an H-F that is leveraged 10:1 a 5% loss in market value turns into a 50% loss in equity. It's not uncommon for an H-F to be leveraged 100:1 with borrowed capital and derivatives. When the market falls 5% or 10%, H-Fs, with this amount of leverage, must liquidate immediately to reduce their loan exposure. Get the drift?

In 1997, Robert C. Merton and Myron S. Scholes received the Nobel Prize in economics for developing a "new method to determine the value of derivatives." Scholes formed Long Term Capital Management (LTCM) and attracted money from tons of investors who, based upon their model trading system, could generate very high returns at minimal risk. Merton was a graduate Ph.D of MIT and is currently on the faculty at Harvard. Both of these men are very smart guys in the field of "financial engineering." Only one problem: in 1998 LTCM lost $5 billion in one day and was on the verge of taking down the entire global equity market. Enter Alan Greenspan, Robert Rubin, and Lawrence Summers—"The Committee Who Saved the World," according to the cover of TIME magazine. No one asked these "maestros" of finance why they allowed it to happen in the first place. I called the three bankers "The 3 Musketeers" in an article I wrote for "We Hold These Truths" magazine.

The purpose of this bit of history? This event in 1998 was a preview to what happened in July 2007. David Rocker, a retired H-F manager, writes pointedly in Barron's "Use of excessive leverage to enhance managers' personal gains should no longer be tolerated. The societal risk is simply too great. Transparency must be increased, and the debate over it should be started now." *ROCK ON*, David![19]

The average person may not understand finance and markets at this level, or what you have read here, but every person needs to understand that what happens on Wall Street does not just stay on Wall Street. It doesn't make lick of difference whether or not you have any money in the stock market ... the fallout from an ultimate implosion of an over-leveraged and *Greed* driven market will impact everyone. The handwriting is on the wall, but the public thinks it's graffiti and doesn't comprehend what the Wall Street gang is up to.

Like Merton & Scholes, Goldman Sachs, the biggest player on Wall Street, devised quantitative-equity or "black-box" strategies that were to produce very high returns with little risk.

Sound familiar?

The pride of Goldman's array of H-Fs is the $9 billion Global Alpha Fund. Seeking "Alpha" is trying to find Alice in Wonderland, as they just discovered. Goldman's Global Equity Opportunities Fund lost $1.5 billion, or 30%, in one week around August 1, 2007. Goldman met its own margin call bellying up to the bar with $2 billion and individual investors adding another billion. How many investors couldn't meet their call in similar funds and lost?

Despite the liquidity crisis and the re-evaluation and write-down of various asset classes, Goldman Sachs reported a 79% increase in its quarterly profit in September 2007. They had a profit of $2.85 billion this quarter versus $1.55 billion in last year's quarter after taking credit for losses of almost $1.5 billion on loans made to fund corporate buy-outs. How could they do that when firms like Citigroup were taking write-downs of $5.9 billion in the quarter and UBS $3.4 billion? Simple: Goldman sold "short" (betting the asset would <u>lose</u> value) on various debt obligations. One could conclude that Goldman knew the subprime debt market would implode, but they wanted to realize the trading profits while at the same time cover their backside.[21]

Not everyone is enthralled with Goldman Sachs. On the 4th of July, 2007, 20 newspapers in New York and around the country received mailed threats against the company hand-written in red on loose leaf paper warning:

"Hundreds will die. We are inside. You cannot stop us."
Signed, "AQUSA"

Idle threats? Cranks? Al Qaida, USA? Who knows? To many observers, Goldman's largess "sucks" up too much money and influence in the world that serves its own interests. There is a growing resentment in America that the rich and corporate America have abandoned the average person and broken the contract with the middle class as indicated above. According to Leo Hindney, Jr. a recently published report of the Horizon Project has identified some of the actions Congress should take. This project brought together eleven CEOs and advisors to address how our nation's global competitiveness can protect the middle class while fulfilling the country's commitment to economic and social fairness. Will corporate America listen and take action? Rather than hope, employees need to press the issue.

Chapter Seven
The Age of Turbulence
(Mr. Greenspan's Perfect Storm)

Tuesday, September 19, 2007, was a bellwether day in America. Former Federal Reserve Chairman Alan Greenspan's book "The Age of Turbulence, Adventures in a New World," was released. That same day an entire nation was on edge, anxiously awaiting the FOMC's decision on interest rates. The irony of Mr. Greenspan's upstaging the latter event shouldn't go unmentioned.

Although appropriately titled, the timing of Mr. Greenspan's memoir[22] doesn't confront the critical issues faced by his successor, Ben Bernanke, and the FOMC by Labor Day, 2007. Prior to addressing these post-publishing events, a look back in time will be instructive. The maroon hard cover of "Turbulence" is stamped in regal gold with the initials AG. I'll refer to the author respectfully by that name.

AG was born in 1926 and grew up in New York City in an area known as Washington Heights. His parents divorced soon after AG was born, and he was raised by his mom Rose, who never remarried. He rarely saw his father, who was a Wall Street Broker. His mother worked as a saleslady in a furniture store in the Bronx during the Great Depression. Despite those perilous days, AG never went hungry and enjoyed an allowance of twenty-five cents per week.

Some sociologists believe that you are where you were at the age of ten. Growing up in a lower-middle-class neighborhood in the midst of the most severe depression and despair the nation has ever experienced must have been a life-defining experience for a quiet, unassuming Jewish kid. To those who were old enough to recall those dire days plus the catharsis of WWII that followed, thrift and fiscal conservatism were values that were difficult to erase. A brave and complex new world, however, lay ahead for AG.

AG admired and read every book he could find on J. P. Morgan. To him, Morgan was "a man of his word," and it was his influence and action that stemmed a bank panic in 1907. AG did not mention that it was Morgan's summer home at Jekyll Island, S.C. that was the scene of the clandestine meeting of global bankers who drafted the Federal Reserve Act of 1913. (Read "The Creature from Jekyll Island," by G. Edward Griffin). Possibly the most significant piece of financial legislation that would impact every American regardless of class was totally ignored by AG.

AG says, "Ayn Rand became a stabilizing force in my life." Who was Ayn Rand?[23]

In 1957, Rand's novel "Atlas Shrugged" was published—all 1,168 pages. As a college student at the time I found it too voluminous and weighty to finish. Rand's novel is a moral defense of the business and concept of capitalism and uncompromising on how government must respect the inalienable rights of the individual in order for business and a society to thrive. She was fiercely anti-collectivist and viewed the bureaucratic central planning of Socialism and Communism as mankind's enemy. Many consider her the founder of Libertarianism. AG says: (p. 53)

"Rand persuaded me to look at human beings, their values, how they work, what they do and why they do it, and how they think and why they think. This broadened my horizons far beyond the models of economics I'd learned."

Another major influence on AG was Adam Smith's "Wealth of Nations," which was published in 1776 in Scotland. AG says the book "is one of the greatest achievements in intellectual history." It answers the most fundamental macro-economic question: "What makes an economy grow?" Smith concluded that to enhance the wealth of a nation, every man, consistent with the law, should be "free to pursue his own interest his own way." Smith's most famous phrase was: "individuals who compete for private gain act as if led by an 'invisible hand' to promote the public good." Smith's invisible hand would not only lead AG—it would mold his core philosophy.

After WWII Smith's theory of a *laissez-faire*, or a hands-off, approach to government involvement in business was not an acceptable concept. The European Socialist countries were highly regulated, and those behind the iron curtain were centrally planned. The U.S. was trying to emerge from a period where all industry was government controlled, which was deemed necessary during the War. Rand's free-market capitalism and Smith's theory in the late 50s were radical thought, but they formed the basis for AG's Libertarianism that would influence him greatly as Chairman of the Federal Reserve.

Retain this thought as we briefly dissect "The Age of Turbulence."

When the term subprime became the neologism *du jour*, the talking heads on CNBC and financial experts assured the public that these mortgages were a small fraction of the overall market, and any problem would easily be "contained." When the contagion spread, the commentators attributed the growing problem to highly leveraged hedge funds and said any perceived crisis would pass. Then when New Century Financial and as many as 100 lenders declared bankruptcy, a global run on the banks followed—not by depositors but by the bankers themselves who made loans to the lenders and had unwittingly bought the CDOs.

In retrospect, home prices probably peaked in late 2005, yet the expansion of the subprime loans dramatically increased in 2006 to $1.1 trillion, up 12% from 2005 (Strategic Investment October 2007).[24] The banks' appetite for CDOs was increasing in 2006 when housing prices were actually declining. The CDO market globally is, as of this writing (October 2007), estimated to be $2.5 trillion. Instead of digging deeper to determine how prevalent the problem was, the "apologists" minimized the situation until the skeletons shook their bones and began to fall out of the closet.

An insight from the inside allows us to see how this all came about. A hedge fund operator wrote a letter to his investors describing how a senior Wall Street marketing director traced the genesis of the subprime market:

"'Real Money (U.S. insurance companies, pension funds, etc.)

accounts had stopped purchasing mezzanine tranches of U.S. subprime debt in late 2003 and [Wall St.] needed a mechanism that could enable them to 'make up' these loans, package them opaquely, and EXPORT THE NEWLY PACKAGED RISK TO UNWITTING BUYERS IN ASIA AND CENTRAL EUROPE!!!!"

"He told me with a straight face that these CDOs were the only way to get rid of the riskiest tranches of subprime debt..."

"This will go down as one of the biggest financial illusions the world has EVER seen."

And despite protestations from a few minimalists, this situation got more grave.

ACA Capital over the past two years has insured $61 billion of predominantly subprime securities which, in the event of the mortgage holders' default, would be the responsibility of ACA. The problem is that ACA has a net worth of only $326 million—a leveraged ratio of 180 to 1. Worse yet, Bear Sterns, Merrill Lynch, Lehman Brothers, and Citigroup have "parked" billions of risky obligations at ACA to obtain capital relief and dress up their balance sheets. Some additional off-balance sheet obfuscations were to follow as noted below.

In Chapter Six above, bank funding of Leveraged Buy-Outs (LOBs) were featured as part of the artificial insemination that made Goldilocks so wantonly desirable. Investment and commercial banks agreed to fund these buy-outs that might not close for six months or so at very low rates (and without escape clauses if market conditions deteriorated, as they did). They planned to peddle these loans to institutional investors after closing. Now they're left holding a bag they don't want and can't sell except at 10% to 12% discounts. Absolute genius! Clear evidence that there has been a paradigm shift in risk assessment by America's banks (noted earlier). Problem is, the bankers don't know which hat they're wearing. In one deal they're lenders; another they're equity partners; another they're fee intermediaries; and another they're investing for their own account. More than occasionally, they're conflicted with conflicts of interest.

Just about the time you think that you've read enough already, another skeleton appears out of the dark. How about SIV?[25]

Virtually unknown even to Wall Street sophisticates are Structural Investment Vehicles (SIV). These creative instruments were set up by Citigroup and other banks as a way to make more money without taking the risk involved onto their balance sheet. Now that the investment estimated to be $350 to $400 billion has turned "toxic," the banks either have to unload them at a substantial loss or move them back onto their books. Remember the off-balance sheet deals that Enron made out of the analytical eye of auditors? Same strategy, different players, but all ethically disadvantaged.

Piled on top of all of the other issues, Citigroup and other banks had a big problem with SIVs. Enter Henry Paulson, U.S. Secretary of the Treasury, [26] with a creative solution. (I often wondered: if the solution is creative, what is the term for the original device?) Paulson recommended a bailout fund (like a superfund for toxic waste) called, of all things, a Master Liquidity Enhancement Conduit (MLEC). A group of banks, even some who had no SIVs, were asked to contribute a total of $100 billion to buy assets from the SIVs. Banks that contributed would earn fees for their support and would also earn fees for trading assets with MLEC. Sounds like the old ditty, "I'm my own grandpa."

The criticism of MLEC was quick and pointed. "I have never seen Treasury play this kind of role," said John Makin, a visiting scholar with the American Enterprise Institute in Washington as well as a principal in a hedge fund. Thomas G. Donlan, the editor of Barron's, was spot on to my early characterization of Goldman Sachs as Goldman Sucks. He states:[27]

The Washington branch of Goldman Sachs, formally known as the United States Treasury, is helping its clients reflate their balance sheets and avoid large write-downs of mortgage-backed securities and other bits of questionable paper."

And Donlan concludes:

"The road to inflation is paved with frightened banks and bureaucrats. Uncle Sugar and Uncle Henry Paulson (former chairman of Goldman Sachs) should stiffen their spines and tell the banks to record the losses they have already incurred."

In a Wall Street Journal editorial making reference to J. P. Morgan (AG's hero) and the Panic of 1907, the editors stated, "J. P. Morgan would make banks write down bad assets." But that was in the olden days.

The MLEC is a desperate ploy to postpone the inevitable and a conspicuous example of the Fed's and now the Treasury's moral hazard.

What in the world is "moral hazard?"[28]

The Fed, under attack from both the political left and the right, has been accused of encouraging Wall Street to take inordinate risks knowing that the Fed will bail them out. It's like building a home in San Diego, knowing that it's vulnerable to fire, earthquake, and mudslide. No one would do it without insurance. Now the Treasury gets into the act in an area which is not within their purview. Wall Street is confident that the Greenspan "PUT," which presumably prevents the stock market from tanking, will be honored by his successor. Alan Abelson, in another of his witty and insightful pieces in Barron's, identifies the new chairman's moral hazard vehicle as the Bernanke "Ka Put."

At the time of this writing, fires were ravaging Southern California. The state, unfortunately, was also the prime target of subprime lenders. The Wall Street Journal[29] analyzed an incredible 130 million home loans over the past decade and discovered that risky subprime loans were made all over the country. Borrowers, surprisingly, were not concentrated amongst low income minorities in inner cities, but high-rate lending also rose sharply in middle class and wealthier communities. The highest concentration of subprime was in California, where 40% of all loans made between 2004 and 2006 were high rate, high risk. Stockton, California has the dubious honor of being the foreclosure capitol of the U.S., where one out of every 27 households are in foreclosure! Not one but two disasters have hit the Golden State at the same time. The financial and humanitarian needs for the state in the next two years could far exceed its ability to provide for them. It will be the "Terminator's" toughest challenge. You may be called upon to contribute.

There is a silver lining in Southern California's soot-filled cloud, however. With 1,800 homes destroyed there could be a mini-boom to builders as homeowners rebuild on their burned out homesites. For those who lost their homes and need quarters immediately, there's plenty of inventory available.

Recently received statistics[30] on foreclosures in the Phoenix Metro area are very enlightening, because they're broken down in median home prices. The data compiled by Dusty Altena at the Arizona Republic also separates the rate of foreclosures from the rates of notices per 80,000 households or those who may soon fall victim to foreclosure.

In the lowest price range (under $200,000) the number of foreclosures per 10,000 households is 41.5, and those receiving notices are 161.1. All of the various price categories separated by $50,000 increments are comparatively similar until you reach the $400,000 to $450,000 class. The rate of foreclosure is 88.9 per 10,000, and those receiving notice are a whopping 224.1. What can be gleaned from this statistical data?

It is generally assumed that the subprime meltdown is primarily occurring amongst the lower income or lower middle class in the lower priced homes. As far as Phoenix is concerned, this appears to be not true. Homes in this price range should fit in the middle class category, assuming that somewhat normal total family income numbers would be present to purchase a home in this price range.

The disturbing trend, of course, is that total foreclosures in the Phoenix area are up 556% through October year-to-date in comparison to 2006. Based upon the current data, approximately 10,000 people will lose their homes in 2007. Of the 50,000 homes listed for sale in multiple listing, an estimated 20,000 are vacant. It's not a pretty sight ... and it shouldn't have happened.

An even more disturbing trend is developing in neighborhoods where there are a large number of vacant homes. In an area called Westview Village in Atlanta, consisting of 85 homes, 22 are vacant. "Now house fires, prostitution, vandals, and burglaries terrorize the residents left in this historic neighborhood ..." says the Associated Press in an article dated November 15, 2007, in the Arizona Republic. Thieves are looting the vacant homes of copper wiring and electrical appliances that can be sold as scrap, virtually making the homes unmarketable.[31]

Supportive of the supposition above, the same AP article reported that upscale neighborhoods are also impacted by the mortgage meltdown. In the Franklin Reserve Neighborhood of Elk Grove, California, south of Sacramento, "a typical home's value has dropped from about $570,000 to the low $400,000s," reports AP, and the area is dealing with the same problems that historically were confined only to inner city areas. More disturbing, however, the AP article reports that the Center for Responsible Lending in Durham, NC estimates that "44.5 million U.S. households will see their property values decline a combined $223 billion as foreclosures surge in coming years ..." That works out to $50,000 per residence! The real tragedy wrought by the MOD cannot and will not ever be determined.

And what about the homebuilders who are after all in the center of this asteroid-filled universe? It seems like just when you think the worst is over, quarterly earnings are released that are equally disturbing. Lennar just reported another write-off of $848 million, and their stock is down 51% year to year. KB Home also took a $690 million pre-tax charge, and their stock is down 45% in the past year. Most of the builder's stock sells at less than ten times earnings which at some point will make them a "buy." Not yet, says Jacqueline Doherty in the 10-01-07 issue of Barron's. "If you're playing the recovery game, she recommends that the deep discounted senior notes of the builders are a better buy."[32]

You're probably asking (and rightfully so): Where the Fed was while this freight train of *Greed* was running pell-mell downhill with no one seemingly interested in applying the brakes? Where was AG, the conductor? I never thought you would ask.

In a "CBS 60-Minutes" interview [33] just days prior to the release of

"The Age of Turbulence," the former Fed Chairman, when asked when he was aware of the subprime lending practices, said "... *I had no notion of how significant they had become until very late. I really didn't get it until very late in 2005 and 2006.*" When one of his Fed governors raised a red flag about these same questionable lending practices, AG replied, "... *we knew there was a number of such practices going on, but it's very difficult for banking regulators to deal with that.*"

Gerald P. O'Driscoll, Jr., a former Vice President at the Dallas Fed and a former director of policy analysis at Citigroup says succinctly: [34]

"The new moral hazard in financial markets has its source in what can be best described as the Greenspan Doctrine. The doctrine was clearly enunciated by Alan Greenspan in his December 19, 2002, speech. Mr. Greenspan argued that bubbles cannot be detected and monetary policy ought not to in any case be used to offset them. **The collapse of bubbles CAN be detected and monetary policy ought to be used to offset the fallout.*"* (Emphasis added.)

This, from a Fed banker, says it all!

While heaping condemnation on AG, why not pile on? My self-appointed mentor of caustic wit, Alan Abelson, the editor of "Up & Down Wall St." in Barron's, wrote: [35]

"Mr. G stands guilty of committing a capital crime several years back (2004) by regaling the peasants, who considered his every word a device utterance, on the joys of adjustable-rate mortgages (as opposed to the old stodgy fixed-rate variety). As it happened, he couldn't have picked a worse moment to make...his 'call to ARMS'." [36]

Responding to these critics and a growing list of protagonists, AG defends his position in his book:

"I was aware that the loosening of mortgage credit terms for subprime borrowers increased financial risk and that subsidized ownership initiatives distort market outcomes. But I believe then, as now, that the benefits of broadened home ownership are worth the risk. Protection of

property rights, so critical to a market economy, requires a critical mass of owners to sustain political support."

What did AG just say? Known for his deliberate obfuscation as Fed Chairman, his well-edited text is considerably more coherent, but he still manages to exploit the grey area.

AG admits (of subprime lending practices) *"I really didn't get it until very late in 2005 and 2006."*

I'm reminded of the story of a fledgling actor who finally got a bit part in a Broadway play. As a large cannon fires a deafening shot on stage, the aspiring thespian was instructed to jump out from behind a curtain and yell "The British are coming!" He rehearsed his line over and over, making certain that his timing was perfect and his elocution conveyed the dire message.

The opening night arrived and the precise moment occurred—a massive "BOOM" rocked the theater! Our erstwhile hero appears on cue—

"What the hell was that?" he cried out.

AG was absolutely right on. He didn't "get it."

Bombs were exploding all over Main Street America ... but like our hero, AG didn't see it and didn't hear it.

AG goes on to say:

"But I believe then, as now, that the benefits of broadened home ownership are worth the risk."

Some analysts are now indicating that up to 50% of all subprime borrowers (2 million) could lose their homes to foreclosure. In addition, those loans classified as "ALT A," the next step up from subprime and "prime," are also showing signs of default distress.

If I'm interpreting AG's statement (above) correctly, despite the fact that half of these homeowners may lose their homes, the remaining 50% who have avoided foreclosure (so far) justify the risk. Let's assume that lenders, investors, and shareholders can absorb the risk of loss of capital. What about the human psychological loss to the homeowners and the social cost absorbed by taxpayers? Is this, on a net/net basis, a gain? I doubt it. In a free enterprise system all the players have a chance to win. Under The

Greenspan Plan, however, half of the subprime participants had the deck stacked against them. Of the other 50%, many took the money and ran.

The last portion of AG's quote can perhaps best be defined as an area neither black nor white, but 'grey:"

"Protection of property rights, so critical to a market economy, requires a critical mass of owners to sustain political support."

A possible translation of AG's "Fed-Speak?"
- There are too many Americans who don't own any property. We can make it easy for them to buy property, but it's up to them to hold onto it.
- We've got to create debt on a massive basis; otherwise it won't be worthwhile.

I have to admit that "to sustain political support" is baffling. Other than the American Dream Down Payment Act, no political support was involved in the Fed's strategy—unless the Fed is "political," which AG vehemently denies. As to AG's intent—your guess is as good as mine.

Criticism of AG from informed sources has greatly debunked the "Greenspan Myth" that has bamboozled the public for 18 years. Circumspection of the Fed and how it operates (or doesn't) has enlightened America. *Greed* will also contribute to demystify the secrets of the temple, I hope. Some very notable names add their insight.

Gene Epstein, who writes "Economic Beat" each week for Barron's, tracks AG as effectively as a bloodhound sniffing out a bank robber. In the March 26, 2007 issue Epstein wrote: [37]

"Meanwhile, try reading Alan Greenspan's 1966 essay, Gold & Economic Freedom, which indicts the Federal Reserve for creating credit bubbles through cheap money. To prevent credit bubbles from occurring, says the then 40-year old economist, the economy needs a system of 'fully free banking...and fully consistent gold standard.' For those who

understand the economy of 2007, the former Fed Chairman has never written anything better."

In "Turbulence" AG doesn't mention how or when his monetary philosophy embracing "a fully consistent gold standard" transformed into a fiat-based monetary system which abhorred the ancient relic of kings. I suspect that the timing may have occurred in August 1974, when AG was named President Nixon's Chairman of Economic Advisors. AG was confirmed on exactly the same day as Nixon resigned—but he stayed on to serve President Ford.

Nixon had instituted wage and price controls (which I remember very well, as my family was enjoying a day of water skiing in New Mexico) and the economy, not to mention the Presidency, was in deep doo-doo. Nixon had abandoned all U.S. dollar ties to gold a couple of years earlier, and my guess is that one of AG's conditions for the job was that he abandon any thoughts of the gold standard in order to be admitted to "Club Fiat" (paper money). By the late 70s (AG was not in Carter's administration), the U.S. experienced the highest inflation since the Civil War. AG ends Chapter 20 of his book by saying, "*... monetary policy should make even a fiat money economy behave as though anchored by gold."* On that account AG failed in both theory and practice.

On September 17, 2007, Epstein was at his best when he wrote:[38]

"The media portray the Fed as a fatherly institution. It is better likened to an odd combination of drug pushers, methadone clinic and rehab."

Quite apt. America has overdosed on cheap credit pushed by the Fed and the MOD. We're now at the methadone dispensing and rehab phase. Many Americans will never recover.

Politicians who eagerly espouse a populist theme have joined the list of AG's detractors. Christopher Dodd (D. Conn.) was reported to have said (Wall Street Journal July 17, 2007[39]), *"They [the Fed] had a job to do and they didn't do it. A lot of people are hurt, and I'm angry about it."* Barney Frank (D. Mass.), who is Chairman of the House Financial Services Committee, has threatened to give some of the Fed's jurisdiction to other regulators if the Fed doesn't begin making changes. Even Mr. Bernanke acknowledged that the Fed had the responsibility *"to prohibit mortgage lending practices that it finds to be unfair and deceptive,"* which calls into question his predecessor's inability to act at the proper time. AG would abhor Congress' meddling, of course.

In early November 2007,[40] the House Financial Services Committee (predicably in response to public outcry) approved The Mortgage Reform and Anti-Predatory Lending Act which as been sent to the floor for vote. This Act imposes a "federal duty of care" on mortgage lenders that will consist of hundreds of pages of regulations that few lenders and their employees will understand but will be obligated to obey. The bill creates a federal cause of action if the lenders won't comply with the law. For example, a borrower can sue for rescission or cancellation of the debt if the court determines that the lender violated any of the onerous provisions of this over-reaching legislation. Imagine for a moment that there could be no foreclosure without a trial. In addition, the Act conflicts with the Community Reinvestment Act which requires lenders to make loans on low income neighborhoods. Its passage could hurt those it purports to assist.

Peggy Noonan writes a column for the Wall Street Journal titled "Declarations." On September 22, 2007, after the release of "Turbulence," she heads her piece "NOW HE TELLS US." She says: [41]

"As a writer I am in passionate support of large advances, but $8.5 million to tell the American people what he should have told them when his views might have had an impact?"

In "Turbulence" AG was diametrically opposed to George Bush's tax cuts. The Bush Doctrine as espoused by Vice President Cheney was "deficits don't matter." Though AG disagreed with the "great pork spree" of the Bush Administration, his congressional testimony was interpreted as supportive of the Bush's fiscal policy which probably secured AG's last term to the Federal Reserve in 2003. Noonan suggests that AG's "oblique phraseology" allowed "partisans to twist AG's words" to suit their purpose, and the Chairman never raised any public objection.

Roasting the former Chairman now serves a vital function for the future. Now that the veil of secrecy of the Fed has been pierced, and the American public can see and understand perhaps for the first time the collusive and manipulative control exercised by Wall Street and money center banks, we the people, who are unwitting victims of its policies, should demand a structural change in the Federal Reserve Bank of the U.S. I realize that this is a quantum leap, but as you'll soon discover in Chapter Nine, a radical and dramatic change in our banking system is already pre-ordained. The opportunity for change will present itself if Americans will seize the day. *Greed* will forewarn and forearm you for the coming battle for America's heart, soul, and wealth that is soon to emerge.

Up to his point many of you are thinking 'Yes, but what about all these greedy bastards who took advantage of the situation and bled the system with no intent of paying the loan? How about the appraisers and the real estate agents and the lenders who colluded together to commit fraud and took the money and ran?' Yes, the era of *Greed* was an opportunity for those who were ethically disadvantaged.

These were the small-time players who sold their soul for $10,000 or $100,000. The Attorneys General for all the states will be busy for the next three or four years tracking down and trying these turkeys. Most will lose their licenses. Some will go to jail. At this time there is no way to estimate how much fraud and abuse occurred, but most of those guilty will get their just desserts.

How about the "flippers" who flipped houses like pancakes? They're heros, in AG's Libertarian view. The winners should be applauded as capitalists, but those caught short when the music stopped shouldn't be given access to a multitude of bailouts coming for those who were the targets of the predatory MODs.

Then there are the big players. Those in pinstripe suits on Wall

Street and the money center banks—the "Robber Barons" of the 21st Century.

Case in point is the story of Stan O'Neal, the CEO and Chairman of Merrill Lynch and Co., who joined Merrill in 1986 in its junk-bond division. In late September 2007 Mr. O'Neal informed his directors that the firm's mortgage losses would be $4.5 billion, and two top bond traders were fired. On October 24 the new bond group came up with a more conservative evaluation of the mortgage write down which boosted the loss to almost twice the original estimate to $7.9 billion. The board, not liking bad surprises, promptly fired Mr. O'Neal. Only the "negotiation" of his severance package was open to question.

At the time of this writing, O'Neal's exit package was estimated at $160,000,000, which did not include any severance pay. While O'Neal's departure was being debated on CNBC, Ron Insana suggested that the former chairman be quizzed about his golf game. It appears that O'Neal was a member of three exclusive golf clubs, and records showed that he had played twenty rounds of golf in the prior six weeks while his world was crashing in around him.

Good point, Ron. Golf in the New York City area is an all-day excursion unless you're in the office at 6:00 a.m. and take the afternoon off. And how can one shift the focus to golf when the penultimate pressure of public scrutiny is about to envelope you? No need to worry. Stan will have plenty of time and plenty of money to play the game now.

Metro PCS Communications, Inc., a Dallas wireless phone service provider, is suing Merrill Lynch charging that its brokers invested $133 million in its ready cash in CDOs. Merrill Lynch advised Metro PCS that the securities were "low risk and highly liquid." Suits of this nature will inundate the court system in 2008.[42]

No sooner had the skittishness begun to settle down over the revelations at Merrill Lynch than the nation's largest bank, Citigroup, [43] became afflicted by the spreading contagion. At the end of October 2007 Citigroup was assuring shareholders and the "Street" that the bank had only a $70 million "indirect exposure" to the subprime mortgage mess. One week later CEO Charles Prince resigned, and the bank admitted looking at somewhere between $8 and $11 billion in write-offs from $70 million. You would think that bankers would be num wouldn't you? Another myth dispelled. But there's one thing you can count on. Be assured that Mr. Prince will not be a pauper as he lies down in green pastures.

Some of the CEOs and CFOs will be expendable. Some in second-tier management will be scapegoats, and they'll fall on swords for their bosses. So, some of these seven- and eight-digit salary guys lose their jobs ... so what? And here's the point—what they *won't* lose: their cushy retirement income and maybe a severance pay package. Stock options and other incentives could stay intact. For some it may be a perfect time to exit the pressure-packed life on Wall Street and move to Arizona (we inherit many of these guys). The bottom line, financially, is that they don't lose unless they end up in court and are guilty of fraud or malfeasance. Is that the way capitalism is supposed to work?

And what about the million of Americans at the bottom of the food chain who lost everything they had? The people whose little home mortgage ended up in a package of CDOs that made this brilliant, creative, ambitious Wall Street Merchants of Debt (MOD) all this money? Has there ever been a time in American history where an elite class has profited so much at the expense of the middle class? I don't think so— not since the exploitation by the 'Robber Barons' of the working class in the early 19th Century.

One of the most egregious instances to develop this point is the story of Franklin D. Raines. Raines was CEO of the Federal Home Loan Bank Board (Fannie Mae) from 1999 to 2004. Wall Street marveled at Fannie Mae's performance under Raines, who was one of their own as a former investment banker at Lazard Freres. Quarter after quarter Fannie met its earnings target. Raines and other officers earned fat bonuses each year based upon the stellar earnings. Only one problem: the earnings were phony! CFO Timothy Howard and Raines had cooked the books, and Raines was finally terminated in December 2004. Fannie Mae had reported

9 billion in earnings that did not exist, and the mortgage lender became severely under-capitalized and almost forced into bankruptcy. So what happened to the ex-CEO?

Powerful friends in high places (he was Director of the U.S. Office of Management and Budget in the Clinton Administration) kept Raines out of jail. His retirement plan valued at $25 million remained intact, and as of this date Raines has not repaid any of the $50 million in bonuses based upon fraudulent accounting.

Then there's that matter of the $36 billion in year-end bonuses paid out in 2006 to senior managers and employees of the five largest investment banks on Wall Street. One young trader in his thirties garnered a bonus of $100,000,000 last Christmas! In case it's difficult for you to decipher or digest that large a number, it is *one hundred million dollars*— to one person.

Surprisingly to some, I will defend and support what has to be an unprecedented amount of compensation. If the young man earned this $100 million bonus based on trading profits, congratulations are in order. If, on the other hand, this trader made his mark on peddling CDOs and subprime debt, he should strongly consider contributing a large portion of this ill-gotten gains to a homeowner's restitution fund. Fair enough?

Unfortunately, cases like Raines are the norm rather than the exception. How and when will this abuse end? Possibly ABRUPTLY— read Chapter Nine.

By late fall of 2007 the "mortgage mess," as the media refers to the subprime catastrophe, two things were abundantly clear:

1. The meltdown was PREDICTABLE, and
2. The meltdown was PREVENTABLE.

I was on record early in 2005 as stating that the real estate boom cycle would come to a halt in 2006 and 2007. I called AG's pending perfect storm "The Great Reckoning." It's difficult to make predictions because they're about the future (if you'll pardon the humor), but my forecast was accurate. Nevertheless, no one wanted to hear that this easy road to riches would soon be full of pot holes.

A bipartisan group in the House of Representatives crafted a regulatory bill in late 2005, but it was derailed by Republican leaders who argued that the market would take care of the problem. The Republicans must also have borrowed Adam Smith's phrase, "Individuals who compete for private gain act as if led by an invisible hand" to promote the public good (page 262). This hand was in the pocket of America's middle class.

Henry Kaufman, the famous Wall Street bond trader and author of "On Money & Markets, A Wall Street Memoir," wrote an op-ed piece in the Wall Street Journal that zeros in on the most critical financial issue of our time. He says:

"The Federal Reserve cannot walk away from its responsibilities to limit financial excesses. The central tenant of monetary policy is to achieve sustainable economic growth.

... It is therefore urgent that the Fed take the lead in formulating a monetary policy approach that strikes the right balance between market discipline and government regulation."

AG has repeatedly said that his first consideration before adopting any policy was "First do no harm." The Fed and the FOMC apparently concluded in 2002 that the "Greenspan Plan," the "Greenspan Doctrine," or whatever title you want to ascribe to the borrow-and-spend policy at its inception, would cause no harm. What did he say in his book after the mortgage meltdown and its aftermath?

"Morever, flexibility and the extent of property rights are related. To obtain flexibility the competitive marketplace must be free to adjust, which means market participants must be free to allocate property as they see fit. Restrictions on pricing, borrowing, affiliations of market practice more generally have slowed growth." (p. 255)

AG is reaffirming his Libertarian philosophy of *laissez-faire* Capitalism that government should not interfere with the free market. AG also adheres to the concept that a marketplace regulates itself through "counter-party surveillance." In other words, the banks or money sources will be restrained on the money they lend if the risk is perceived to be too great. In the present case AG would conclude that the investment banks (like Merrill Lynch), the commercial banks (like Citigroup), and the mortgage companies (like New Century Financial) will take their hits, hopefully survive, and live on to participate in the next boom. To a Libertarian, that is acceptable to me unless there is the potential for systemic failure. We were damn close by Fall 2007. And it ain't over yet as 2008 is off to a rocky start.

As we have just experienced, the commercial paper (short-term notes issued by corporations to meet short-term needs) market became illiquid in August 2007. There were no bids to buy. The market was frozen. Why? No one could determine the value of all the CDOs. AG's book was probably on its way to the printer at the time of the liquidity crunch, so he didn't have to address the issue of systemic risk or the failure of the banking system in "Turbulence."

Henry Kaufman addresses this issue in the same op-ed piece quoted above.[44]

"And their [the banks] reach into the financial system is so broad and deep that no central bank is willing to allow the collapse of one of these leviathans. They are deemed too big to fail ... If some institutions are really too big to fail, then other means of discipline will have to be found."

Where will that discipline come from? If the Fed doesn't assume that function, you can be assured that Congress will find a way to intercede. The subprime meltdown has created a wave of "populism" where citizens demand relief and Congress will make an all out effort to appease the masses in exchange for votes.

In his last Chapter, AG assumes the role of the Oracle at Delphi and peers into the future to the year 2030. None of his forecasts are particularly earth-shattering or ground-breaking save one. The Chinese word for crisis also spells opportunity:

"Markets have become too huge, complex, and fast moving to be subject to twentieth-century supervision and regulation. No wonder this globalized financial behemoth stretches beyond the full comprehension of event he most sophisticated market participants ... We (Fed) increasingly judged that we would have to rely on counter-party surveillance to do the heavy lifting."

Greenspan is out. Bernanke is in. Will the "bearded one" be governed by the same Libertarian philosophy? Does he have any choice? His mettle was tested early, and he could be facing issues that even the "oracle" could not have imagined or articulated.

To the reader of *Greed*, Bernanke's departure from his predecessor's philosophy of *laissez-faire* will come as a shock and reward the author with "just desserts."

In an article "Fed Targets Abuses in Home Loans"[47] by Jeannine Aversa of the Associated Press, the writer reports that the Fed will propose new rules that would apply to all types of lenders including brokers to be effective after January 1, 2008. The rules are:

1. Bar lenders from penalizing subprime borrowers who pay their loans off early.

2. Force lenders to make sure that borrowers set aside money for taxes and insurance.

3. Restrict loans that do not require proof of borrowers' income.

4. Examine lenders' failure to consider proof of a borrowers' ability to repay a home loan.

5. Curtail abuses in mortgage advertising.

Collectively, let's all respond to the Fed's and Mr. Bernanke's initiatives:

DUH!

The observations are obvious, but for the record they should be memorialized here:

1. Mr. Greenspan maintained that the Fed had no authority to propose rules governing the mortgage sector, when it is clear it did.

2. The proposed rules come three years too late. The horse has already bolted from the barn. Few, if any, lenders are going to be inclined to make subprime loans—until the next boom (Chapter Ten).

3. Mr. Bernanke has "dissed" his predecessor and mentor, Alan Greenspan. AG's legacy now becomes shrouded by the inevitable question: *Why didn't you, Mr. Chairman, foresee the problem and take this action?*

So, what else can we expect as 2007 comes to a close?

Mortgage guru Jeffrey Gundlach, the CIO of Santa Monica, California-based TCW Group, sees the housing woes getting much, much worse in what he calls "the great margin call of 2007." Home prices, he says, "could drop an average of 12% to 15% annually from the highs achieved last year and not reaching their eventual trough until late 2008 at the earliest."[48] Grundlach sees an unprecedented opportunity. TCW has already raised $1.6 billion for a new "vulture fund" to buy distressed mortgages.

Congress has recently passed legislation that creates a $100 million fund for non-profit groups who will counsel delinquent borrowers. You can expect a new "cottage industry" to emerge that could employ thousands of real estate agents who haven't had a closing in a year. Massachusetts has sold bonds to raise $250 million to help struggling homeowners refinance to a fixed mortgage. The state of Arizona and other states sued Ameriquest Mortgage Co. for predatory lending and won a $325 million settlement. Arizona's share will be returned to more than 14,000 homeowners. Many "Zonies" are faced also with as much as a 50% increase in real property taxes ... an additional dilemma faced by many property owners. [49]

On August 31, 2007, President Bush offered up the Federal Housing Administration (FHA) to help homeowners to refinance their ARMs and to temporarily relieve them of income taxes on forgiven debt. (Congress passed legislation to prevent taxation on a "short sale" which will be effective for 2007 and will expire December 31, 2009.) Homeowners have been shocked to learn that a 'short sale' to the lender for less than the principal mortgage is taxable income. It's a form of "phantom income"—taxable, but no cash. It appears that President Bush didn't bother to check with Senator Susan Collins (R) of Maine, who had supervised a Senate Subcommittee investigating mortgage fraud.[50] Senator Collins concluded that the Federal government through the FHA had essentially subsidized much of this fraud. The FHA insurance fund to pay off defaults is now exhausted, and taxpayers will be called upon to ante up.

As *Greed* was in the process of its final rewrites and editing, the Bush Administration was close to an agreement with the mortgage industry to freeze interest rates on more than 2,000,000 subprime loans that will reset to higher rates in the last quarter of 2007 and all of 2008. The "freeze the teaser" plan. The point man for the Administration's New Hope Plan is Secretary of Treasury Henry Paulson. Under The Plan, only a limited number of borrowers would qualify for assistance. Those in foreclosure, more than 60 days past due, or more than 60 days delinquent over the past year will not qualify for help. The implementation of The Plan could be a nightmare. Now that government and the Fed has had to interfere in the crisis and become "hands on," maybe AG could offer a revision to "Turbulence" in a second edition. Fortunately for the "Maestro," there are no more book signings and embarrassing questions from a less-than-admiring public.

Randall W. Forsyth, in his column "Current Yield" in the December 3, 2007, edition of Barron's,[51] appropriately summarized the government's involvement in the Administration's plan to freeze interest rates:

The same spirit of forbearance would seem to inform the White House to stave off rate increases on ARMS to some borrowers while the markets cheered, this proposal would amount to defining delinquency down ... for those who are unable to pay."

The subprime mess has attracted capital from foreign investors and sovereign wealth funds. Abu Dhabi infused $7.5 billion in cash into Citigroup, our nation's largest bank, and will receive 11% on their money when market interest rates are substantially below that yield. Abu Dhabi also took an 8% stake in Advanced Micro Devices and a 7.5% stake in the P-E firm Carlyle Group, which also lists the Bush family amongst its investors (see Chapter Nine). It seems that the Committee on Foreign Investment in the U.S. (CIFIUS), which up until recently had raised objections for national security concerns (like Dubai Ports Worldwide), has suddenly become mute on recent deals. The soft underbelly of Uncle Sam has been exposed—another example of how our bankers have placed all America at risk.

And finally, the sharks smell blood in the water. In Ohio, which has one of the highest home-foreclosure rates in the nation, a young attorney has seized an opportunity to get into the very deep pockets of Wall Street. Marc Dann, Ohio's Attorney General, "has sued more than a dozen lenders and brokers for allegedly inflating home appraisals and engaging in other practices that misled troubled homeowners."[52] His principal focus, however, is on Wall Street and the credit rating companies cited earlier who made the CDOs marketable as AAA bonds. It's probably a career maker for the ambitious Mr. Dann—much like his hero, Eliot Spitzer, now Governor of New York.

So how does this subprime mortgage fiasco compare with other past debt crises?[53]

Year	Crisis	Losses/Billions	As a % of GDP
2007	Subprime Mortgage Losses	$150 to $400 (est.)	1% to 3%
2000-2003	Tech Bust Bond Defaults	$93	0.9%
1990	S&L Crisis	$189	3.2%
1982	Bank Loans to Developing Countries	$55	1.7%

The history of the U.S. banking system is punctuated seemingly every ten years or so by bubbles. There must be a genetic flaw in the bankers that lies dormant for long periods of time which suddenly comes to life when triggered by a herd instinct in search of *Greed*.

These numbers, of course, do not include the write-down in real property values. The article cited above estimates that approximately $6 *trillion* worth of housing wealth could be wiped out as a result of the subprime mess. In the stock market crash of 2000 to 2002 a similar amount of perceived wealth evaporated. The difference here is that the homeowners' equity or perceived wealth could also disappear, but in most cases the asset still remains with a large note attached to it. The winner of the annual Mensa (those with genius IQs) Invitational Contest for a new descriptive word has a new definition applicable to the current real estate market:

CASHTRATION: The act of buying a house which renders the subject financially impotent for an indefinite period of time.

According to Irvine, California based Realty Trac, Inc., 446,726 homes nationwide were targeted for foreclosure from July to September 2007, up 100% from the same period one year ago. The firm expects the numbers to increase in 2008. Given the foreclosure numbers to date and the dire projections from 2008 and beyond, where does the responsibility lie? Who are the players at fault in the blame game? Thomas G. Donlan, the Editor of Barron's, says it's easy this time since "Seldom have so many been so deserving."[54]

1. *Alan Greenspan and George Bush.* Their contribution has been well chronicled here. Bush's tax cuts and "The Greenspan Plan" were stimuli worthy of democrats, and together they were too much.

2. *Bill Clinton and his promoters at the Department of Housing & Urban Affairs, Henry Sisneros and Andrew Cuomo.* It took a long time to get the housing boom started, and they were the originators.

3. *William R. Fair and Earl J. Isaac*, who started a credit analysis company that was used in three out of four mortgage originations. They turned credit from a character judgment into a commodity. Fair Isaac was a key ingredient in the mortgage mess.

4. *Standard & Poors and Moody's bond ratings*, as mentioned earlier. The bond issuers paid handsomely for AAA ratings that were strewn with junk.

5. *The predatory lenders such as New Century Financial, their phony appraisers and brokers* whose goal was to create as much debt as their conscience would allow—which conscience had no limit. And finally,

6. *The American public who borrowed imprudently, should have known better, and who are now seeking relief from the populists who thrive on their grist.*

Donlan and his staff at Barron's are, in the opinion of this writer, the best at what they do in search of truth. I've relied heavily on their research for this book. You would serve yourself well by subscribing to their newspaper online or in print.

Chapter Eight
The Future Isn't What It Used To Be
(The Unexpected is Now)

As a history buff and a political and economic pundit, I've become fascinated with the similarities between the "Roaring Twenties" and our era of *Greed*.

The 1920s were considered a time of great prosperity in America when technology ushered in a modern era. The Federal Reserve Bank of the U.S., after its rebirth in 1913, had amongst its stated goals two that were extremely relevant to this period. One, Americans were especially thrifty savers, particularly during World War I, and the Fed was intent on creating an environment of consumerism to boost the economy by spending; and two, the promoters of the newly created Central Bank assured Congress and the American public that bank panics and depressions of the past would never reoccur. The Fed succeeded in its first mission and, of course, failed miserably in its second.

Henry Ford created the assembly line and mass produced the Model T, which made the car affordable to the working class. Radio was the technological wonder of the era, as were a myriad of electrical kitchen appliances. The one key ingredient that made Americans shop and spend was *consumer finance*. Americans for the first time could purchase homes, autos, furniture, and gadgets on credit. Excessive easy credit would also end badly in 1929, as it has today.

President Warren G. Harding (elected in 1920) became an advocate of Adam Smith's *laissez faire* economics, and his government "hands off" policy allowed capitalism to thrive. Opportunists and cronies in his administration also prospered, and Harding's term in office was marked with scandal, corruption, and profiteering. (Remember the "Tea Pot Dome" scandal.) AG's strict adherence to *laissez faire* also ended an era fraught with fraud and corruption.

Excess credit and rampant speculation plus the "extraordinary popular delusions and the madness of crowds" led to the stock market crash of 1929. In the '20s investors could borrow up to 90% against their portfolio—which exacerbated and accelerated their margin calls when the crash occurred. Excess leverage, whether it be in stocks, commodities, real estate, or any asset class, is the helium that inflates all bubbles. De-leveraging and re-pricing of assets is the hallmark of 2007 and 2008. We should all hope and pray that our current recession does not become the Great Depression of the '30s. More on this in Chapter Ten.

America became isolated after World War I. Just prior to the war, the U.S. was processing and admitting approximately 1.0-1.5 million (legal) immigrants per year. In 1924 Congress passed the Anti-Immigration Act, which limited immigration from countries where 2% of the total U.S. population per the 1890 census (not counting African Americans) were immigrants from that country. Asians and citizens of India were excluded completely. The massive influx of Europeans (my parents and grandparents included) who came to America in the two decades after the turn of the century slowed to a trickle. Eighty years later America is faced with the same dilemma—whether or not to close its borders.

The '20s were also referred to as the "Lawless Decade" immortalized by Al Capone, John Dillinger, Bonnie and Clyde, "Bugsy" Moran, and others. The Eighteenth Amendment to the U.S. Constitution was enacted in 1920 which prohibited the manufacture, sale, import, and export of alcoholic beverages. This Act, known as Prohibition, created a fertile opportunity for gangsters to profit from illegal endeavors through "Speakeasies," smuggling, and various other nefarious activities. The comparison to gang activity today is quite apparent. Substitute drugs for alcohol, and the battle for "turf" and market share are synonymous. Today's gangs are equally well organized, armed, and brutal. The principal difference is that Al Capone and his ilk warred with his rival gangs and the police. Today the M-3, Mexican Mafia, and other gangs target American citizens as well as their competitors and have overwhelmed our police, our resources, and our ability to rid our society of this menace.

Remarkably, the '20s was an era of social liberalism. There was an acceptance of gays and minorities. William Haines, widely acclaimed as the top movie male box office draw, openly lived in a gay relationship with his lover, and gay social clubs were known as "pansy clubs." A hit song of 1926 was "Masculine Women, Feminine Men." Mae West wrote a popular play about homosexuality called "The Drag" which was a box office success. Homophobia resurfaced in the '30s and persisted until late in the 20th Century.

Minority acceptance was probably best exemplified in the arts—particularly in music. The '20s was also known as the "Jazz Age"—a term coined by author F. Scott Fitzgerald. Jazz, an improvisational and highly sophisticated harmonic idiom, stemmed from Black spirituals sung in previous centuries in West Africa. Jazz first began to evolve along the Mississippi River in the U.S. In the early '20s it migrated to Chicago and then to Harlem in New York City, where it became extremely popular and would influence all American music to the present. One of the jazz ages's most visible stars was Louis (Satchmo) Armstrong. Eighty years later, Black America would create another original musical medium—Hip Hop.

Any mention of the "Jazz Age" would have to include the "Flappers." Origin of the term has been long deliberated, but it definitely came to identify impetuous teenagers or women up to age 30 who went to jazz clubs at night, where they danced provocatively, smoked cigarettes through long holders, sniffed cocaine, and drank 'hootch' in open violation of Prohibition.[55] The flappers were promiscuous and shocked observers with suggestive dances such as the Charleston, the Shimmy, the Bunny Hug, and the Black Bottom. The flappers have their counterparts today in Paris Hilton, Lindsay Lohan, and teenage girls who are "grinding" and "freak dancing." The Flapper era ended abruptly when the stock market crashed in 1929. Will history repeat itself? Will teenage and young adult behavior today, so reminiscent of the '20s, grind to a halt? Poverty would create a moral revolution.

America today has a couple of other noteworthy high-profile connections to this unforgettable era. The Black Sox scandal, where a number of Chicago baseball players were accused of throwing a World

Series, created a black cloud over America's favorite past-time until the "Babe" brought the fans back to the stadiums. Barry Bonds and others who are suspected of using steroids to enhance their performance have also cast a shadow over the game, which could also result in a life-time ban for this super-hero and others.

This era also produced strong women who were determined to change their image and station in life. Margaret Sanger wrote "The Woman Rebel" in 1914, which had a direct impact on the creation of the liberated woman of the '20s. Today America has a strong but polarizing woman who may be the first American female president.

All of the comparisons above are but a prolog to the supposition that the American economy of today has eerie similarities to the "Roaring Twenties."

There are a number of theories as to the cause of the "Great Depression." I subscribe principally to the Austrian School of Economics' theory postulated by the late American economist Murray Rothbard, who believed that government manipulation of the money supply sets the stage for a series of boom and bust cycles as outlined in Chapter One. His view was that the Federal Reserve's over-expansion of the money supply in the '20s led to an unsustainable credit boom that rapidly inflated asset prices—particularly stocks and capital goods. By the time the Fed began to raise interest rates and tighten credit in 1928, the mania had gotten out of hand ... and the stock market crash of October 29, 1929, was inevitable.

Rothbard, as well as other monetarists, Milton Friedman (who passed away in November 2006), and the current Fed Chairman, Ben Bernanke, believe that the Great Depression that followed the crash was caused by monetary contraction and persistent bank failures when panicked depositors made a "run on the banks." During the first ten months of 1930, 744 banks failed—and by the time the 1930s ended, approximately 9,000 banks in the U.S. had closed their doors. There was no deposit insurance in this period, so most customers lost a good portion, if not all, of their money. When the euphoria and *Greed* of the "Roaring Twenties" was overcome by the all-pervasive fear in the '30s, the U.S. economy contracted and remained depressed until December 7, 1941.

Herbert Hoover took the blame for America's greatest economic failure, but in reality it was the Fed's over-expansion of credit and money supply that created the boom. Equally as important, it was the failure of the Fed to proactively intervene after the bust occurred that caused the Great Depression to continue for eleven years. The prolog is similar, the epilog is in question.

There is ample evidence that there is more than just an eerie connection between today and the '20s. The boom of 2002 to 2006 has turned to bust. The only question that remains is: will our bust of 2007 become a recession—or worse, a depression? In the '30s there were two social classes—the haves and the have nots. Opulence and despair. Are we again witnessing the destruction of America's middle class? Stay tuned.

Those of us who were born in the late '20s and the '30s were children of "The Greatest Generation"—a term made famous by Tom Brokaw in his 1998 book by the same name. It was dedicated to those who fought for America's freedom in WWII. The heroic deeds of our parents during this entire decade of despair known as The Great Depression should include this era. My father and mother, who married in 1928, had just begun a life together full of optimism and hope—but, unfortunately, for them and 200 million Americans, THE FUTURE WASN'T WHAT IT USED TO BE.

My sister was born at the onset of the Great Depression. I was born in 1936 in the midst of it, and my brother was born at the end of the worst deflation the nation has ever known. Amongst family mementos I have a small invoice from Bellin Memorial Hospital in Green Bay, Wisconsin for my mom's (and my) four-day stay during my birth as a testimonial to those hard times. The hospital charge was *five dollars per day*! I wrote *Rediscovering America, Growing Up in the Forties"* as a tribute to my family and to preserve a time soon to be forgotten—the "Golden Era" in America following WWII.

Fast-forward to 1960 and my graduation from the University of New Mexico in Albuquerque. My first non-summer job was in Los Angeles selling credit cards (noted earlier in Chapter Six) for Hilton Carte Blanche. While on a training session early in my development my manager remarked that he could sign up just about everyone he encountered as we proceeded to work our way down Sunset Boulevard in Hollywood. As we encountered a well-dressed, conspicuously affluent gentleman walking his dog, my manager introduced himself and began his sales pitch. The gentleman was very receptive, even eager to apply for a card.

"Your full name sir?" My manager asked as he pulled out an application.

"Meyer Cohen," the gentleman responded. "But I'm best known as Mickey,"

I was a pretty green kid from New Mexico, but I suspected that "Mickey" was probably the infamous gangster. Shortly after this encounter, Mickey went to jail for the third time in 1961 for tax evasion. Not surprisingly, Hilton rejected his application but my manager was right— you can approach anyone just about anywhere. Thus began a sales career where I would encounter many interesting and iconic people.

I relocated to Los Angeles principally to train for an attempt to qualify for the U.S. Track & Field Team that would participate in the Olympic Games in Rome late in the summer. With a second-place finish in the National Collegiate Athletic Association Championship (NCAA), a second in the National Amateur Athletic Union (AAU) Championship, and a gold medal and record in the Pan American Games all in 1959, I was considered a favorite to win a spot in the javelin on the 1960 team. My original plan was to enlist in the U.S. Marine Corps and train with my teammate and world record holder, Al Cantello, but I failed my physical exam.

The Navy doctor correctly assessed my physical limitations. I struggled with a congenital back problem for several months into the 1960 season but regained my form just prior to the finals when three athletes would be chosen for each event. It wasn't to be. In the AAU championship in Bakersfield, California, in which I needed to finish in the top six to make the Olympic qualifying meet, the javelin judge ruled that my first two throws were flat (the point didn't strike first) and the third was out of bounds. Any of the three would have easily allowed me to qualify for the trials, but I never got the chance. I attributed my failure to "the fickle finger of fate." Disappointed but undeterred, I sought other challenges and joined my father, who was the manager for a life insurance company, to begin my chosen career.

I started at $300 per month, which was an advance against future commissions. My principal source of prospects were college friends who were married and starting a family. They all needed health and life insurance. A typical hospital and surgical plan for a family of four was about $12 per month. Today, a family of four could pay $1,200 per month for a high-deductible plan—an increase of 10,000% in a span of forty-seven years. No one on this planet in the '60s projected that medical costs, prescription drugs, and health insurance would reach these astronomical levels, far outpacing inflationary forecasts.

In 1961, the maximum tax base for Social Security was $4,800, of which I paid approximately $150 in social security tax and my employer matched an equal amount. (There was no Medicare tax until 1966.) For my clients, Social Security provided a solid base benefit at a reasonable cost for the working head of family who would die prematurely and leave minor children. No one questioned the actuarial projections or the future solvency, viability, or cost of Social Security. It was the cornerstone of all financial planning and as secure as the name implied. So it seemed.

Fast-forward to 2006. Olivia and I receive $35,000 per year in retirement benefits from Social Security. Eighty-five percent of that income was taxable. The taxable base was $94,200, and the tax rate was 6.2% in 2006. Medicare has no ceiling or limit, and the tax rate is an additional 1.45%. We currently pay over $15,000 in Social Security and Medicare taxes, which is almost 50% of the retirement benefits. Add state and federal income taxes to the 85% that is taxable as income, and our total tax outlay is almost equal to the income received. We just received notice from Social Security of "Modified Adjusted Gross Income." Based upon our total income in 2006, Olivia and I will pay an additional premium for Medicare.

Named MAGI, this is the first "Means Test" that will be incrementalized in the future. Based on *your* retirement income, you will be asked to pay more for your benefits and/or receive a cut in benefits. That should get your attention. If not, read on.

Here's how Social Security has worked for us (and most of you). We've contributed almost $150,000 of our own money to the fund, and an equal amount has been paid by our employer (mostly by our own corporation.) There isn't a trust fund established in our names for these contributions, and if we were killed together in a plane crash, none of our money passes to our children. We don't have control over our own money. Congress controls it, and the politicians have spent virtually 100% of our money. For the privilege of using our money they've given a non-negotiable IOU to the Social Security Administration that carries a below-market interest rate averaging about 2%. It's no wonder Congress doesn't want to reform Social Security. They might lose control of the (cheap) money:

Your Social Security Statement (if you haven't read it carefully) carries the following warning:

ABOUT SOCIAL SECURITY'S FUTURE ...

Social Security is a compact between generations. For more than 60 years, America has kept the promise of security for its workers and their families. But now, the Social Security system is facing serious future financial problems, and action is needed soon to make sure that the system is sound when today's younger workers are ready for retirement.

Today there are almost 36 million Americans age 65 or older. Their Social Security retirement benefits are funded by today's workers and their employers who jointly pay Social Security taxes—just as the money they paid into Social Security was used to pay benefits to those who retired before them. Unless action is taken soon to strengthen Social Security, in just 14 years we will begin paying more in benefits than we collect in taxes. Without changes, by 2042 the Social Security Trust Fund will be exhausted.* By then, the number of Americans 65 or older is expected to have doubled. There won't be enough younger people working to pay all the benefits owed to those who are retiring. At that point, there *will be enough money to pay only about 73 cents for each dollar of scheduled benefits. We will need to resolve these issues soon to make sure Social Security continues to provide a foundation of protection for future generations as it has done in the past.*

**These estimates of the future financial status of the Social Security program were produced by the actuaries at the Social Security Administration based on the intermediate assumptions from the Social Security Trustees' Annual Report to the Congress.*

This message from Jo Anne B. Barnhart (The Commissioner of Social Security) is dire, but it's actually sugarcoated. As you are about to discover, the problem is much more complex and costly than this statement suggests. The corrective urgency is *now*. As in the past, politicians and policy wonks will continue to defer any viable solution until the crisis is undeniably upon us. It wasn't supposed to be that way in the future.

A future consisting of a longer life span, designer drugs to mitigate disease in advance of its onset, and a more healthy lifestyle has to bring comfort and joy to those who haven't already pondered what lies ahead. So, what's the problem?

We didn't expect to live that long. It wasn't supposed to be that way, and:

THE U.S. FEDERAL GOVERNMENT CAN'T AFFORD TO PAY THE ENTITLEMENTS THAT WE EXPECT TO RECEIVE.

These entitlements—Social Security, Medicare, Medicaid, and other benefits—are paid by the government. Taxpayers are the funding source. That's you and me. You've read the Commissioner's warning. The following information which is taken from The Coming Generational Storm: What You Need to Know About America's Economic Future by Lawrence J. Kotlikoff and Scott Burns [56] and cuts through the political rhetoric to provide us with the truth on a subject that will impact all of us.

In the Fall of 2002, the then U.S. Secretary of Treasury, Paul O'Neill, requested a study for inclusion in President Bush's FY2004 Budget of the federal government's long-term liabilities. Dr. Kent Smetters, an economic professor at the University of Pennsylvania and presently serving in the Treasury Department, and Dr. Jagacleesh Gokkale, who was serving as a senior economic adviser to the Federal Reserve Bank of Cleveland, undertook the herculean task. The two decided to measure the "fiscal gap"—the difference in present value between the government's receipts and future expenditures, assuming future generations faced the same tax net rates as current generations.

The fiscal gap was calculated at a mind-boggling $45 trillion. The total net worth of all of the American people according to the Federal Reserve is $40 trillion. Technically, the country is bankrupt—but that's not the principal story.

The obvious question is: What would it take to deal with this massive and expanding shortfall? The economists came up with the following "Menu of Pain:"

Policy	Percentage Change
Increase Federal Income Tax	69%
Increase Payroll Taxes	95%
Cut Federal Purchases	100%
Cut Social Security & Medicare	45%

Apply the magic of compound interest and wait fifteen years when half of the Boomers have reached retirement age, and the $45 trillion problem grows to $76 trillion. Add the Medicare drug benefit already passed by Congress, and the $45 trillion fiscal gap becomes $51 trillion!

Now here's the shocker:

President Bush, running on a platform that called for tax cuts in 2004, didn't cotton up to Secretary O'Neill's fiscal report and, like kings in the past, if you don't like the message, kill the messenger. Secretary O'Neill was fired. More significantly, the Gokkale and Smetters report was expunged from the Congressional Record. Taxes have been cut, and the fiscal deficit and the mammoth funding problem confronting Social Security and Medicare have been pushed ahead to the future. Social Security's fiscal gap is *three times worse* than the public has been led to believe.

Author's Note:
On December 17, 2007, David Walker, a Director at the U. S. General Accounting Office (GAO), at a speech at the National Press Club, admitted that the unfunded liability was $53 Trillion, up $20 Trillion since 2000. He also admitted that the government can't possibly meet the liability.

Where is the generational conflict? Kotlikoff and Burns say that "We find that future generations face a lifetime net tax rate that is twice the rate we're (presently) paying." A rising life expectancy and lower birthrates are the two principal drivers in the aging of the planet. And I suspect, but don't know, that the full potential impact of the Human Genome Project is probably not factored in these financial projections.

The greatest demographic change in world history has already caught us. The population over age 65 will double in the next 30 years. At present there are 60,000 people in the U.S. age 100 and over. By 2050 this number will exceed 600,000. At this same time the "old" will exceed the young for the first time in history. To say that Social Security and Medicare are under extreme financial pressure is a gross understatement.

For the past 30 years, members of both political parties have bowed to the "grey panthers," the power of the AARP and other political action groups, and secured and preserved the benefits of current retirees. By the use of "generational accounting," securing today's benefits are accomplished by reducing the benefits of future retirees. The political policy of this country has been to indulge the present at the expense of children and the unborn. As the authors quip, "This gives new meaning to 'taxation without representation'."

So, who is going to foot the bill?

The children of the Greatest Generation now in their 60s and 70s. My generation.

We will, as a group, get back more in benefits than we have paid in taxes—if we live at least five years or so after drawing benefits at age 65. In the 1960s our parents spent, on average, 9% of their remaining assets each year to live on. Today we, and the children of my parent's generation, spend about 14% of their resources per year. As a group we have more assets than our parents, but our costs to maintain our standard of living are higher.

According to Katlikoff and Burns there is another major shift amongst my generation. Our children (the Boomers) will inherit substantially <u>less</u> than has been projected. The bumper 'snickers' say, "Retired—Spending My Children's Inheritance." It's shorthand for "I've done my bit. My kids can take care of themselves ... Spend `til the end ..."

<u>The Boomers</u> (1946-1964). The 77 million children of my generation. According to a study done before the stock market crash in 2000 by Robert Avery and Michael Randall, $14 trillion would pass from my generation to the Boomers. Gokkhale and Kotlikoff did their own study and proclaim the $14 trillion as a hoax. Their conclusion? "... baby boomers are not going to be able to rely on inheritances to finance their retirement to a greater extent than their parents."

The Boomers are faced with a number of unprogrammed challenges, most of their own making. At present the total tax bite during their highest income years is the lowest that they will experience in their lifetime. The tax bill will increase significantly—and soon. This generation, as a group, has not been savers. They're consumers. They have bought into the Greenspan Plan and have utilized the cash-out refinance plan to the max. They're highly leveraged (in debt) and are not prepared for what looms ahead. Most importantly, they've assumed (incorrectly) that their taxes will decrease at retirement.

<u>Generation X</u> (1965-1981). The precise time frame isn't established, and this generation was without a name until Paul Fassell in his book titled

Class called this group of people who wanted to hop off the merry-go-round of status, money and social climbing the "X'ers." A British punk group took the name in the 70s, and their image as shockers and drop-outs branded their fans and contemporaries. One universally accepted belief of the X generation is that they will never see Social Security in their retirement years. What the X'ers haven't caught on to yet is the taxation without benefication—their contributions are mandatory to keep the system afloat without assurance that benefits as now promised will be there.

The New Millennials (1982-). The oldest of this unique generation is now graduating from college and entering the job market. They are as distinctly different from the "X'ers" as night and day. They believe that it's "cool" to be smart and successful. They've been raised on technology and learned to multi-task most of their lives. They gravitate toward group activity and collaborate well in reaching goals. They're extremely impatient, and their greatest asset could be their desire to change the system so poorly developed and managed by their parents. Freed from the past, they're the hope for the future. They will quickly recognize the incredible challenge that awaits them.

Do Kotlickoff and Burns have a solution? Yes! And, it makes perfect sense. They call it the PERSONAL SECURITY SYSTEM (PSS). "It's far too late to escape the generational storm, but there's still time to get out of its direct path ..." say the authors. The problem is that it requires convincing the American people that are facing grave economic crisis. But it's easier to convince the public of what they want to hear: The problem doesn't exist. The bottom line is, we shouldn't expect a material effort to reform Social Security—and every moment increases the urgency to do so. MOST importantly, this information should motivate all of us to reassess our current retirement plan to protect ourselves. The future has moved our cheese.[57]

*Author's Note: As the manuscript of **Greed** was in the process of being submitted to the publisher several initiatives have been proposed that would have a dramatic impact on Social Security.*

According to Barbara J. Kennelly, President and CEO of the

"National Committee to Preserve Social Security & Medicare,"[58] *a bill named HJ Res. 1 proposes a Balanced Budget Constitutional Amendment that, if passed, "could impose constitutionality-required cuts on Social Security and Medicare spending and threaten future benefits." Given Congress' penchant for prolific spending, it's difficult to believe that the majority required for an Amendment to the Constitution could ever pass, but it has connoted the severity of the problem documented here.*

In another mailing piece (from Phyllis Schlafley, organizer of the Eagle Forum), the writer claimed that the Council on Foreign Relations (CFR) has "demanded" that President Bush allow illegal aliens from all countries to participate in America's Social Security system. The plan is called "Totalization" and would allow all illegal aliens to receive benefits within 18 months of entry into the plan.

Back to my career. Within a year I was my dad's best agent in New Mexico, which was more a reflection on the lack of ambition and professionalism of my cohorts than my level of success. Suddenly and unexpectedly (to me), my father was fired by the company that he had loyally served for 30 years—which occurred within a year of his qualification for full retirement as a branch manager.

Dad's *faux pas* was two-fold. One, he dallied with his office manager, and two, his office wasn't productive. I found myself in a quandary when I had to morally support my mother and continue to work for my dad with his girlfriend running the office until the end of 1961. Not exactly an atmosphere in which to excel. Financially, for my dad to lose his retirement income of almost $20,000 per year was devastating. Two years later Dad, who had divorced my mom and married his office manager, had a son and at age 57 had to start at ground zero selling life and health insurance.

Occasionally, the "fickle finger of fate" chooses to smile upon us. January 1, 1962, was one of those rare, life-defining moments in my life. On a ski trip to Taos (New Mexico) Ski Valley and a brief chance encounter on New Year's day, I met a very attractive, sophisticated lady, smartly dressed in a waist-length mink jacket, matching hat and tight-fitting red Bogner ski pants. I was smitten—by an "older" woman by the name of Olivia Savage, the mother of two incredibly intelligent and well-manner children—Susan, age five, and Mark age four. After an eight-month courtship (we didn't "hook up" in those days), we were married on August 22, 1962. Olivia was then a student at the University of New Mexico after being out of school for 10 years, and she would complete her BA, her MA, and work toward her Ph.D in English literature after we were married.

After two years in the direct package sale of life insurance, I knew I could succeed in the business—but there had to be a more professional method and career rewarding opportunity. I found it at the Connecticut General Life Ins. Co. (CG), which at that time was the sixth largest life insurance company in the U.S. and exclusively featured comprehensive estate planning training for its representatives. I complemented my extensive training in Denver at CG by returning to the University and audited both estate planning and income tax courses. Good fortune soon opened another door of opportunity that would quickly propel me to become one of the top sales reps in the country with CG.

CG was one of the foremost agribusiness lenders in the U.S. boasting an established relationship with hundreds of farmers and ranchers in New Mexico and West Texas. These entrepreneurs had large net worths and very little liquidity. The estate tax exemption then was a mere $60,000, and tax rates quickly reached 50%. I convinced a reluctant management that I was the man to work exclusively with the farm and ranch loan office in Lubbock, Texas, doing estate planning for the company's existing borrowers. My agribusiness sales experience then was my spouse, who was born and raised on a ranch in Southeastern New Mexico. It worked.

Here's the reason for imposing on your time and patience to tell my story and my relationship with this special class of people.

James P. Owen is a 35-year veteran of Wall Street. He is an owner/partner of Austin Capital Management in Austin, Texas, and its Director of Corporate Values. Jim is the author of the financial bestseller, *The Prudent Investor: The Definitive Guide to Professional Investment*

Management and *The Prudent Investor's Guide to Hedge Funds: Profiting From Uncertainty & Volatility.* For the focus of our discussion here, I will refer to his 2004 book *Cowboy Ethics: What Wall Street Can Learn from the Code of the West.*[59] Below is the author's purpose for writing this book—and it was prior to the ethics scandal documented here in *"Greed."*

Author's Note
Why This Book

After thirty-five years in the investment management industry, I can tell you that it runs on brains, nerve, and ambition. This business doesn't often give you the chance to do something from the heart. But I am taking that chance now, because the subject of our industry's ethics and values has become my consuming passion.

Not so many years ago, the denizens of Wall Street inspired awe and envy. We were "masters of the universe" and had the numbers to prove it. But after a wave of scandals exposed a dark side of the industry, I found myself mourning what had been lost. I could only wonder: How did we get to this sorry state? When did we stop caring about our principles and the well-being of our clients? And most importantly, how could we begin to redeem ourselves and earn back the trust of investors and regulators? Our malady was so deep-rooted that I could see no cure.

A little more than a year ago, almost by accident, my troubled musings on the state of our industry came together with my lifelong interest in the Old West and the era of the open range. Suddenly I found my source of inspiration: the real-life working cowboy. I spent the next year exploring the life and code of the working cowboy and distilling the principles of what I call Cowboy Ethics.

Spreading this word has now become my calling. In fact, I see it as the culmination of my career; I feel as though everything I have ever done has led me to this point. While I am still an active partner in my firm, a hedge funds advisor based in Austin, Texas, my career emphasis has shifted.

Now when I think about how I would like to be remembered, it is *not as the guy who lived in a beautiful house or brought in a lot of business or helped to build investment firms—though I have done all those things. I would rather be known as the guy who was not embarrassed or afraid to speak up about issues that matter a great deal. I have come to realize that anybody can make money; it is much harder to make a <u>difference</u>. That is what I hope Cowboy Ethics will do.*

By no means is Cowboy Ethics the last word on Wall Street ethics; I am not that naive. But I am optimistic. I believe Cowboy Ethics can be a profound source of inspiration for meaningful change that starts with individuals, percolates through firms and organizations, and could ultimately help transform the industry at large. Wall Street desperately needs a way out of its morass. Cowboy Ethics is a place we can start.

James P. Owen

Santa Barbara, California

Owen defines the "Code of the West" in his own list of ten principles that capture its essence. John Wayne has probably demonstrated and quite possibly articulated each one of the ten in all of his films. Writers about the west and their heros have exemplified them. To the cowboy, The Code was unwritten, but he knew what it was and abided by it. Owen's ten principles are:

1. Live each day with courage.
2. Take pride in your work.
3. Always finish what you start.
4. Do what has to be done.
5. Be tough, but fair.
6. When you make a promise, keep it.
7. Ride for the brand.
8. Talk less, say more.
9. Remember that some things aren't for sale.
10. Know where to draw the line.

To those of you who know the west and have observed the life of the true working cowboy, these principles are clear, irrefutable, and true. For those of you who have only viewed the west from afar, from a comfortable chair in a movie theater, or from a recliner while reading a Louis L'Amor novel, Owen's amplification and application of The Code will be enlightening and instructive.

Danger is the cowboy's companion everyday. One of my friends was run over by a bull in a remote pasture and lay their helpless and in pain for an entire day before he was discovered. Another (who was age 80) was thrown from his horse against a water tank, severing his carotid artery. Both of these contemporary cowboys survived to work another day. But as Owen says about courage, *"It is also willing to speak up and say something that is right—even if that means going up against partners, colleagues, or superiors."*

The boardrooms of Merrill Lynch, Citigroup, and all the Wall Street firms cited earlier needed someone with the courage to tell the now-deposed CEOs that profiteering from CDOs was unethical and wrong. Quite possibly there was a "cowboy" on their staff, but they refused to listen. Stanley O'Neill, in particular, surrounded himself with only those who agreed with him.

Despite the fact that the subprime mortgage mess had not surfaced when Owen's book was released on "The Code," he had some timely advice. "But on days when things seem especially tough, I think about what it must have been like on an open range in the middle of a blizzard, and I tell myself 'cowboy up'." One of the other admonitions *apropos* is "When you're riding through hell ... keep riding." Another is, "Cowboying doesn't build character. It reveals it."

To many of us John Wayne was **"The Cowboy"** and epitomized The Code. He certainly was "tough but fair." Owen uses this except from Wayne's last film, *The Shootist* (1976), to illustrate this point. "I won't be wronged, I won't be insulted, and I won't be laid a hand on. I don't do these things to other people, and I require the same from them." The authentic golden rule was not the one who had the gold or makes the rules in the cowboy code of ethics.

"Ride the Brand" has a particular significance today. In the olden days it meant the cowboy's loyalty to his employer. Owen makes a key distinction in today's world. "If you work in the investment industry, make no mistake about where your loyalties should lie: The client comes first—not when it's convenient, not when you feel like it, but always!" Wall Street has long abandoned this principle of The Code—if they ever honored it.

The author has a very pointed message for the Street in Rule 9: "Remember That Some Things Aren't For Sale." Owen says, "Our industry is known for being full of smart people. But think about it: How smart can we be if we don't value our reputation above all else?" Owen has highlighted one of the main reasons why there has been, and will continue to be, a customer exodus from Wall Street firms by investors managing their own money.

The final—and to me the most significant—rule to live by is, No. 10, Know Where To Draw The Line. "There's right and there's wrong, and nothing in between," as the book relates.

I encountered that "line" after I sold my three-state insurance brokerage operation in 1978 and became associated with a small investment banking firm specializing in the merger and acquisition of small cap companies. Working on a number of transactions with an associate within the firm, I withdrew from any further prospective deals because of this individual's lack of professionalism and unethical behavior. I was chastised by the owner of the firm: "Buster, the problem with you is that it's either black or white—there's no grey area."

The owner was telling me that the deal was the paramount consideration. I would have to bend and compromise with people if the deal was to come together. My personal code of ethics didn't permit operating in the grey area, so I left the firm. Certain events occurred later that clearly demonstrated that those who do not embrace The Code are destined to suffer the consequences.

By 1963, armed with my technical skills and an entre to those ranchers that still lived by The Code, I set out to make a career in this 'niche' market. In most cases I was able to bond quickly with these folks who had a great need. They were faced with an enormous tax liability at death, and it was up to me to gain their trust and deliver on my promise to create for them and their families security through the preservation of their estates.

My travels soon took me to Plainview, Texas, where two brothers had a large cotton farming operation, a large net worth, considerable debt, no financial or estate planning, and no insurance. Their roots were planted in The Code ... but as I was about to learn, there were those in agribusiness who did not live by it.

During my third meeting with the brothers I wrote a $1,000,000 life insurance application on each of them, which is comparable to about five million in today's dollars. We were sitting in their unpretentious office sipping Cokes spiked with Jim Beam (Plainview is located in the Bible Belt, and liquor was prohibited) when a black Cadillac limousine rolled into the parking lot enveloped in a cloud of West Texas dust. The chauffeur got out and opened the door, and out stepped a seemingly out-of-place businessman dressed in a Hickey Freeman (or comparable brand) sharkskin suit and alligator cowboy boots.

"Well I'll be damned," said one of the brothers, "if it ain't ole' Billie Sol."

Despite the fact that I had no idea who Billie Sol Estes was, the flamboyant entrepreneur was already a legend in Texas. At that point in time Estes had already been convicted of fraud over his illegal acquisition of cotton allotments—receiving over $20,000,000 per years in payments from the Department of Agriculture. He was regarded as somewhat of a hero amongst the farmers with whom he did business because of their distrust of the government and its and interference in their businesses. I didn't think too much of my chance meeting that day until later that year when John F. Kennedy was assassinated in Dallas and there was a link made between Billie Sol and the newly elevated Vice President Lyndon Johnson to the Presidency. If you think you've heard all the conspiracy theories of JFK's death, Google Billie Sol Estes and be prepared to be dumb-founded.

What is important for our purposes here is the revelation of the wide disparity of business ethics from the working farmers and ranchers at the core of the agribusiness industry to the promoters and the government officials at the top. I was a strong supporter of JFK but could never "cotton" to LBJ when I learned of the code by which he lived.

When Olivia and I married in 1962, we rented a very unpretentious home only a block from her previous residence for the modest sum of $125 per month. Within two years we were able to purchase a brand new 3,500 square foot, tri-level, five bedroom, four bath home only two blocks away for the incredible price (in terms of today's prices) of $35,000—ten dollars per square foot. The 5%, 30-year fixed mortgage required a payment of $288 per month. I was personally interviewed by the President of the Savings & Loan and several loan committee members prior to the commitment. There were 20 kids the same age as our children living in our small subdivision, and the school was only a block away. It was a perfect place to raise a family that was about to expand to three children (son Hunter arrived in October). No one in those days thought of their home as an investment to 'flip' and uproot their family. Our investment in our home was for the security, comfort, and stability of our family.

As the 60s progressed, my business prospered and expanded geographically as far as San Antonio, Texas, the Oklahoma panhandle, Southern Colorado, and all of New Mexico. I purchased a Cessna 182 Super Skylane so I could cover the wide open range faster and more efficiently. I used my plane as you would an automobile, landing on dirt roads, in pastures, and even occasionally at airports. The ever-present high (30 to 40 mph) winds of the high plateau country were a challenge, but it was the unknown risks that could be the killer.

My client J. Casper Heimann, whose headquarters were at Hayden, New Mexico, referred me to an adjacent neighbor, Sam Whiteside. Sam was only ten minutes away by plane, near Bueyeros, New Mexico, and was waiting for me below outside his pickup in a pasture marking the best spot for a landing. Approaching to the west at about 200 feet off the ground and at about 100 mph, I was focused on the windmill and determining the wind direction when suddenly as if the good Lord tapped me on the shoulder I looked straight ahead and discovered I was on a direct 90 degree collision course with—a U.S. Air Force B-52 Bomber! Both pilots were staring directly at me, probably praying I would see them. I could see the pupils of their eyes!

Instinctively and instantly I jerked the stick back into my lap and my plane leaped vertically 90 degrees. As my stall warning blared, the wing of the monster bomber passed beneath me! I pushed the stick forward and regained sufficient air speed to avoid a stall. Wings level again, I looked to the east and watched this massive plane continue its mission, stirring up a vortex of dust at the end of its wings because of its close proximity to the ground. I had survived instant death by a matter of seconds. God and good fortune would be my constant companion for all these 71 years.

The B-52 was assigned to the Strategic Air Command (SAC) at Roswell, New Mexico. Their training mission was called an "oil burner route" marked on air maps where the crew was instructed to fly at 200 feet off the ground. Still, who would expect to come face-to-face with this behemoth (which obviously couldn't change its direction at that altitude) out in the middle of nowhere? Not too long after this incident my friend J. witnessed a fighter jet on the same route doing a belly roll that crashed on his ranch. J. and his sons were injured when compressed air tanks exploded at the site.

By the end of 1965, my dad had relocated to Roswell (where SAC was) and was, ironically, working on the base selling insurance to servicemen. Then the government closed the base. In a long, gut-wrenching, emotional, typewritten letter my father revealed to me that he was broke with a young son and desperately needed my help. On January 1, 1966, I organized Insurance Consultants, Inc, made Dad its president, and paid him the same amount that he would have received in retirement pay if he hadn't been fired, plus a car and benefits. He solicited surplus business from casualty agents and agents who worked for other companies. It was a perfect fit for him, and within a year he and the new business thrived. I was one of the first insurance agents in the country to obtain a security license and began to expand my personal business to include investments.

The late 60s saw my first experience with "extraordinary popular delusions and the madness of crowds." The investing public was pouring money into mutual funds appropriately named "go go funds." New to the business, I, too, thought nirvana had been discovered. Never in the history of the U.S. (there were only a smattering of mutual funds in the "Roaring Twenties") had the small investor experienced growth rates of 20% a year or more. By 1970, the bubble had burst. I vividly recall that the Enterprise Fund lost almost 50% of its value from its high in 1968, and it took five years for it to regain its net asset value. Fortunately, ranchers were—and still are—as patient as Job, and their equity was restored.

One of Insurance Consultants, Inc.'s creative and successful programs was marketing health and life insurance to depositors of rural banks with the bank sponsoring and participating in the program. In the fall of 1969 we were working with a bank in Socorro, New Mexico, 70 miles south of Albuquerque. Dad and I had been sharing the same motel room but had to split up since we had to go through a switchboard to set our appointments for the next day. One of my associates and I were discussing our work progress one evening in his room when Dad said:

"You know, they shut off the switchboard every night at 10:30 p.m. What would a person do if had to make an emergency call or something?"

Sensing that Dad was somewhat anxious about not having his oxygen available (Dad had a rheumatic heart condition), I replied:

"Are you not feeling well, Dad? Do you want to go to the hospital and get on some oxygen for awhile?"

"No, no, I'm okay. It's Friday, tomorrow I'll be home," he stated somewhat unconvincingly.

Dad didn't make it through the night. When he failed to arrive at the bank in the morning, I knew instantly what had happened. I could hardly breathe as I drove back to the motel. Most people instinctively know when the end is near. When you're age 33 and haven't had anyone close to you pass away, you don't heed the warning signs. Dad was only 65.

Certainly I failed to act, and I should have insisted that I drive him to the hospital. He would have survived and probably lived a number of years more. But I do have the satisfaction that I came to his assistance when he needed me most and those last four years he was productive and happy. My half-brother David's sixth birthday was the day of our dad's funeral. As the fickle finger of fate would have it, ten years later David would come to live with me and Olivia after my stepmother's death. My son and my half-brother (nephew and uncle) were only one year apart in age.

By 1972 Insurance Consultants, Inc. had optimized its growth in a state with only approximately one million population. I was weary of the extensive travel and had several additional near misses flying in the countryside, so I sold my plane and made the decision to expand the brokerage business to Phoenix. My original intent was to open an office with a local Phoenix partner, but he made a decision to go it alone at the last moment ... and since I had committed to office space, I went forward with my expansion plan. Attracted by the fabulous weather and the dynamic business environment, I made the decision to permanently move to the "Valley of the Sun" in 1974. Chapter One begins with that defining moment in our lives. In so many respects, I discovered, as you have,

The Future Isn't What It Used To Be.

Chapter Nine
The Oracle at Phoenix
(A View From Outside The Box)

The last chapter in Alan Greenspan's book, *"The Age of Turbulence,"* is entitled "The Delphic Future." It's the former Fed Chairman's projection of global events to the year 2030. It's curious that AG draws from a reference to Greek mythology to render his forecasts. Since we now recognize that the future isn't what it used to be, the question remains: *What is* the future?

Delphi,[60] which Olivia and I have visited and at whose significance we have marveled, is located in lower Greece and is best known as the site dedicated to Apollo during Greece's classical period. The Priestess of the Oracle at Delphi (who took the name of Pythia) sat on a tripod over an opening in the earth and, possessed by Apollo's spirit, prophesied the future. Reminiscent of AG, the Oracle spoke in riddles that only the Priests of the Temple could interpret for the people who came to her for counsel on all matters. I'll attempt to play the role of a "priest"and interpret AG's prophesies. The "Oracle at Phoenix" will conclude this book with his own forecasts through a mythological connection.

Apparently AG was using Greek mythology to demonstrate that "People have always been enthralled by the notion that it is possible to peer into the future." Nowhere, perhaps, would this ability be more desirable than the prediction of stock prices. Unfortunately, however, "... financial crises that are foreseeable by market participants (including soothsayers, I presume) rarely happen." As an example AG says, "The horrendous decline in stocks on "Black Monday" October 19, 1987, came out of the dark."

Really?

AG must have forgotten that it was Elaine Garzarelli, who was managing a fund of $500,000,000 at Shearson Lehman, and others who concluded that the stock market was 35% overvalued at that time. She went to 50% cash in her fund and bought put options for insurance one week prior to the crash. The event made her a heroine to her investors and the most visible analyst on Wall Street. Even your humble author also saw "Black Monday" coming, and I wasn't even involved in the equity market as an advisor at the time. "Out of the dark?" I don't think so.

Rather than prognosticators moving markets, AG agrees with this author and says it is human behavior that's the ultimate culprit. "When gripped by fear, people rush to disengage from commitments, and stocks will plunge. And when people are driven by euphoria, they will drive up prices to nonsensical levels." Like 1996 when AG made his most famous (or infamous) utterance which he says he will never live down: "How do we know when irrational exuberance has unduly escalated asset value which then become subject to unexpected and prolonged contractions?"

These words precipitated a sharp sell-off in the stock market on that day. Though short-lived, irrational exuberance prevailed and accelerated until March 2000 when the .com bubble finally burst. AG says the bubble was building four years before it burst, but did little to quell the exuberance. Nothing was learned from this experience.

I get a sense that AG is reiterating his mantra of *laissez-faire* capitalism without explicitly repeating it. His "irrational exuberance" proclamation may have given him pause that he should not interfere to quell the exuberance when, again, the Fed had provided the helium for the bubble. But (and here is the key fundamental question) if AG truly believed in *laissez-faire*:

Why did the Fed intervene in the first place? Why did the Fed feel compelled to jump start the economy in 2001 but then not intervene when speculation got out of control?

So here we are at the end of 2007, at the onset of a recession or worse, and populist demand is clamoring for draconian government intervention in the mortgage mess. An opportunity for government to 'socialize' or nationalize the housing sector is a distinct possibility through massive bailouts or takeovers of borrowers and lending institutions including the twisted twins Fannie Mae and Freddie Mac. It is also an opportunity for Socialism to retain its unblemished record of never achieving success.

AG would like us all to be investors like his friend Warren Buffett and others like him who are "willing to endure the angst of watching their net worth fluctuate beyond what Wall Streeters call the sleeping point." Market volatility—another word for fluctuation—is a trademark of the times. Why? In the opinion of this author, we don't have free markets anymore. Fundamentals are virtually meaningless when government, investment bankers, and special interests have the ability to manufacture economic data, have the leverage and the capital to move the market to suit their purposes, and have the influence and power to control a democratic society. A number of years ago Julien Robertson, who formed Tiger Management, a hedge fund that averaged a compound average annual return for his investors of 32% from 1980 to 1996, closed all his funds at the end of the tech bubble, declaring that the stock market did not make sense anymore—a reference to irrational exuberance and market manipulation.

Quite possibly Robertson's lament is one of an old warrior trying to do battle in the 21st century with weapons from WWII. Or, as AG says, the markets will become "too huge, complex and fast moving to be subject to twentieth century supervision and regulation." They could also become, by 2030, too large to manipulate. Whatever the case may be, the immediate challenge is now upon us. No one predicted that a small obscure sector of the mortgage market could bring down the strongest economy the world has ever known—but it has. Humpty Dumpty has had a great fall, and it's up to all the King George's horses and all of King George's men to put him back together again. *Not* a comforting or reassuring thought!

AG muses about the U.S. economy in 2030. There are a number of preconditions that he requires before any projections can be made, but the most significant is the nature of our rule of law. "I do not believe most Americans are aware of how critical the Constitution of the United States has been, and will continue to be, to the prosperity of our nation."[61] I couldn't agree more with AG but find his assertion curious when you consider what is soon to unfold in the possible formation of the North

American Union (NAU).

AG is a consummate insider. He is a member of the Council on Foreign Relations (CFR) whose goal is to subvert the U.S. Constitution to a higher authority. Our rule of law, unique in the world, will be subordinate to a new constitution of the NAU just as those twenty-seven member countries of the European Union now find themselves. Long before 2030, I suspect that the transition to the NAU will be complete (unless citizens revolt) and textbooks in our public schools will be purged of any reference to the U.S. Constitution and the Bill of Rights. The former chairman is being just a little disingenuous when he states "The Constitution ... will and continue to be [critical] to the prosperity of our nation."

One of AG's prognostications has already come to pass. He says, "But the dysfunctional state of American politics does not give us great confidence in the short run. We could instead see a return of populist, anti-Fed rhetoric, which has lain dormant since 1991."[62] AG wouldn't want to acknowledge that strong criticism would come from former Fed members condemning the "Greenspan Doctrine," but it has.

AG goes on to say,

"I regret to say that Federal Reserve independence is not set in stone. FOMC discretion is granted by statute and can be withdrawn by statute. I fear that my successors on the FOMC, as they strive to maintain price stability in the coming quarter century, will run into populist resistance from Congress, if not the White House."[63]

Henry Paulson, the U.S. Secretary of the Treasury, was the first to cave in to populist demand from Congress and Wall Street and presented the "Freeze the Teaser" as a solution to the mortgage mess. Pressure from various other sources has already caused Ben Bernanke to aggressively move to lower the Fed Funds and the Discount Rates. Well aware of the perfect storm the Fed had created prior to his retirement, the current ground swell of populist demand for government intervention was an easy forecast for AG to make. His "I told you so" may even be an attempt to deflect the eventual and inevitable blame from himself.

A Phoenix[64] is a mythical bird which has its origin in ancient

Phoenician mythology as well as Egyptian, Greek and Christian lore. At the end of the bird's life cycle, its nest ignites and both the nest and the bird are reduced to ashes. A new young Phoenix arises from the ashes. Christians use the myth as a symbol of Christ's resurrection. For our purposes here we're using the myth to designate the Arizona city which claims the mythical bird as its namesake and is the nest of the author.

The forecasts of the future by AG (through the Oracle at Delphi) are considered by this author to be from "inside the box." There is no question that AG's superior intellect, his background and experience at the highest level of global finance, and his thorough understanding of the political system undoubtedly qualifies him to write such a book and make these forecasts. But unfortunately, AG cannot, by virtue of the very position he commands, apprize his reader with what he really knows. He can't think "outside the box."

I want to speak to you objectively and directly, without any stylistic prose.

As 2007 draws dejectedly to a close, the Fed, the FOMC, and the entire banking industry find themselves in a quandary of their own making. The nation is on the brink of a recession. Americans are overwhelmed and overburdened with a mountain of debt that they cannot service. While all the media focus is upon the mortgage mess, defaults in auto loans, credit cards, and student loans are rising at an alarming rate. What could the Fed, these gatekeepers of our monetary system and our markets, have been thinking? Was the total amount of debt they created irrelevant? What course of action do they take now?

Ever since August 2007 the Fed has injected hundreds of billions of dollars into the banking system to provide liquidity to a commercial paper market frozen with fear. A consortium of central banks in Europe plus Japan have agreed to make a massive infusion of money, via an auction, into their banking systems to encourage their banks to make more loans. Additional lowering of the Fed Funds rate and the Discount Rate will further weaken the U.S. dollar, exacerbating the rise in commodity prices—thereby increasing the cost of essentials while income is declining. The

Fed's tools to avoid a recession are cheaper money and easy credit. They've run that string out. To whom will the banks lend to restimulate the economy? The Fed and its member banks have painted themselves into a corner, and it could take a long, long time for the sticky paint to dry. As one wag put it, "Why did the bankers come up with a new way to lose money when the old way was good enough?"

I will conclude *Greed* as the "Oracle at Phoenix"—my own projections of what may occur by the year 2030. These musings of an "old bird" are not simply intended for shock value. Their purpose is to prepare you for the unexpected which, in the opinion of this author, will offer both challenges and opportunities. May the good Lord and good fortune be your companion for the rest of your life.

The North American Union

The Oracle at Phoenix will defer to one of the foremost experts in the U.S. on perhaps the most invasive and poignant social, political, and economic change facing America in the immediate future—the merger of the United States, Mexico, and Canada into The North American Union.

Jerome R. Corsi is a Harvard Ph.D and author of several books and many articles including "The Late Great USA,[65] which is a well-documented and researched exposé on "How globalist business leaders and taxpayer funded academics are deliberately side-stepping the Constitution and Congress in order to submerge the U.S. into a regional government."

Ludicrous, you say?

It's conceivable that over 90% of the U.S. population has never heard of the terms The North American Union, The Security & Prosperity Partnership, or the new currency that will replace the dollar—the Amero. Perhaps up to 75% of the readers of *Greed* have never heard of these seemingly far-fetched concepts, and it's almost a certainty that most Americans haven't fully grasped the ramifications of this titanic shift that will end the America that our founding fathers created 230 years ago. I implore you, please, read Jerome Corsi's book regardless of your political persuasion and regardless of whether you agree or disagree with the concept of "globalism," which is an a-political movement.

Corsi profoundly and effectively quotes from Abraham Lincoln's Gettysburg Address that "the Civil War was a test of how long a nation 'conceived in liberty, and dedicated to the proposition that all men are created equal' could endure." Lincoln also stated that the U.S. is to be a government "of the people, by the people, and for the people." Lincoln's short speech captured the historic significance of America. It is the America of Lincoln and the America that all of us have known that may not endure. It's the government of the people whose rights were endowed by God that may "perish from the earth." It's America's sovereignty that may be subordinated to a regional government controlled by an elitist few. If you dismiss this greatest threat to America as the rant of "kooks," you'll be relegated to the same class of hundreds of millions of Europeans who now find themselves a subject of the European Union.

Although the European Union had its conceptual origins back in the '40s, the actual Treaty of the European Union was signed on February 7, 1992, uniting twelve countries (now twenty-seven) under one flag. On January 1, 2002, the Euro was introduced, and all of the currencies of the twelve countries became collector's items. An EU passport now allows all citizens to more freely across all borders and live and work in any country they wish. The globalists had achieved all their objectives until the French and the Dutch came to the conclusion that if they voted in favor of the EU Constitution it would mean that they would completely lose their sovereignty and be controlled by a limited number of elitist multinationals. A coalition from the left and the right refused to ratify the EU Constitution. Corsi believes that "The EU movement would have been dead before it started" if many of the large nations had known that the Treaty of Rome signed in 1957 would have led to the loss of self government.

The North American Free Trade Agreement (NAFTA), effective January 1, 1994, was the preamble to the present all-out effort to fast track the North American Union by 2010. That's two years from now! Up to this point proponents of the NAU have used the strategy of incrementalism and secrecy to forward their cause. Corsi says, "The movement toward a North

American Union begins with the economy, moves to the courts, and ends with political union. It's a simple story, and one that's taking shape right under our noses."

As early as February 16, 2001, President George W. Bush and President Vicente Fox of Mexico met at Fox's ranch in Mexico and developed a concept of a "prosperity partnership" between the two countries. This became the "Security and Prosperity Partnership of North America" (SPP) after 9-11, which then included Canada. After a meeting of the leaders of the three countries in Waco, Texas, on March 23, 2005, "The Waco Declaration" was issued declaring the three countries' participation in the SPP, and it has been on a fast track since that date. It's important to note that the SPP was never submitted to Congress for debate. No law was passed by Congress or signed by the President, and no treaty ratified by the Senate. In fact, the leaders of the three countries didn't sign anything, thereby avoiding any scrutiny. "Working groups"—a code word for bureaucrats, were assigned the task of developing a report on the SPP and responding in ninety days to the leaders of the three countries.

"On the day the North American Monetary Union is created— perhaps on January 1, 2010—Canada, the United States, and Mexico will replace their national currencies with the Amero —"

Herbert G. Grubel
"The Case for the Amero" 1999

Who is Herbert G. Grubel?

He is a heavyweight in Canada. Grubel is an economist with the Simon Fraser Institute in Vancouver, British Columbia. He has a Ph.D. in economics from Yale University and has taught at Stanford, the University of Pennsylvania, and the University of Chicago. He was a member of the Canadian Parliament and has published twenty-seven books. He has an extremely influential voice in international economics. He's the man who coined the term "Amero."

As I have outlined earlier, the U.S. dollar has devalued against all the world's major currencies with the exception of the Mexican peso. The decline has been persistent and gradual, but continued devaluation could precipitate a dollar crash. A dollar crisis is now quite possible. One could make a case that a collapse of the dollar has been programmed by the bankers and the globalists in order to facilitate the acceptance of a solution—the Amero.

Texans more than any other Americans are the best informed about the globalist's plan for the NAU. The NAFTA super highway (aka THE TRANS TEXAS CORRIDOR)—four football fields wide, from the Mexican border at Laredo to the Canadian border north of Duluth, Minnesota, is rapidly becoming a reality. (Google NAFTA Superhighway—there are over 200,000 links). The purpose for this massive distribution system? Import cheap Chinese goods into Mexican ports, avoiding U.S. union-dominated ports in California; truck the goods without inspection to a Mexican-operated port in Kansas City, Missouri, and then distribute the goods to all points in the U.S. and Canada.

A pipedream, you say?

The Texas Department of Transportation (TxDOT) has an expedited means of acquiring the land necessary for the right-of-way. A new Texas law allows a "Quick Take" eminent domain authority to seize a property within 90 days after a landowner is served with an official notice of a "Quick Take." There will be no protest or recourse by the landowner. Corsi states that one million landowners could be impacted, literally destroying farms and ranches and dissecting communities.

On March 11, 2005, the TxDOT signed a "Comprehensive Development Agreement" to build the TTC-35 (Trans Texas Corridor) with a limited partnership consisting of Cintra Concessiones de Infraestructuras de Transporte, SA (a Spanish company) and a San Antonio, Texas firm, Zachary Construction Corporation. When completed, U.S. citizens will pay a toll to a foreign company that will lease and manage the highway. Other states are joining the parade to sell infrastructure to foreign countries—a trend that will expand in earnest all over the U.S. In case you haven't seen the sign, America is for sale.

An interesting "insider" sidelight: in 1992 President George H. W. Bush signed an Executive Order which allowed states and cities to lease public works infrastructure to private investors, making the TTC-35 deal possible. It isn't a coincidence that Mr. Bush the elder is an investor in the Carlyle Group, a global private equity firm that purchases and builds infrastructure projects. Dubai International Capital and Move-On.org (funded by leftist financier George Soros) are also investors in Carlyle. When it comes to globalism there is no discernible difference in political parties or even foreign entities that may have terrorist connections.

There are a number of inconspicuous ironies that may not surface if and when the NAU debate takes place. NAFTA was intended in part to provide jobs for Mexico's working class (remember Ross Perot's giant sucking sound?) and lift them from poverty as the U.S. outsourced manufacturing to the Maquilladoras. Those Mexican jobs were soon diverted to cheaper labor in China, and the Mexicans sought work in the U.S.

The strong dollar policy initiated in 1994 accelerated the loss of millions of manufacturing jobs in the U.S. over the past ten years. The middle class in America, as cited earlier, is being squeezed by sharply reduced earnings and rapidly increasing cost of living. The globalists are promoting the import of cheap goods to a middle-class market that is finding it more and more difficult to pay for essentials. Wal-Mart's blue-collar customer base is made up of many of those who have lost their jobs to globalism, an irony that has gone un-noticed. I can remember the billboards featuring Sam Walton with the inscription "We buy only American products."[66] (Sam is probably rolling over in his grave over what the folks in charge today have done to his promise.)

As globalism inexorably expands, I couldn't help but reflect back to my college days when I first read George Orwell's *"1984."* Written in 1948, Orwell envisioned a totalitarian world consisting of three super-states: Oceania, Eurasia and Eastasia. Altering the geography a bit, Oceania would be the North American Union that would eventually incorporate

Central America and South America. Eurasia would be the European Union excluding Asia. Eastasia will ultimately be China's hegemony of all of Asia, including Russia —annexed either by force or merger.

The Inner Party of "1984" would be the Elites which Orwell saw as 1 to 2% of the population. The Outer Party would be the upper middle class consisting of about 13% of the population, and the remainder will be the "Proles" (the proletariat). Big Brother already exists in the form of photo surveillance on street corners, in banks, stores, and the soon-to-come biometric ID. My favorite analogy is the Ministry of Truth which would be in the NAU the Bureau of Labor Statistics. Idiocy? The subliminal signs of "1984" are everywhere:

> *War IS Peace*
> *Freedom IS Slavery*
> *Ignorance IS Strength*

In the New World Order everything will be reversed.

Globalism will be sold to you and all Americans as a path to economic prosperity—a tide that will lift all boats (except submarines). But make no mistake about it, free trade is simply the "hook." Free trade is an oxymoron. Not long after agreements are signed there are quotas, tariffs, duties, taxes, and other forms of devices to "level the playing field." What the globalists seek is absolute control—not too different from Orwell's perceived global threat of Stalinist Totalitarianism. To the educated elite like Herbert Grubel and the super-rich elite like David Rockefeller, the Outer Party and the Proles shouldn't have a policy voice in the New World Order. We simply don't have the acumen to comprehend global governance and are a deterrence to it. But we do have numbers, and if those numbers don't assert themselves soon, our voice will be relegated to an ineffective whimper.

A groundswell is gathering to prevent the NAU from becoming a *fait accompli.*[67] On January 22, 2007, Rep. Virgil Goode (R. Va) introduced House Concurrent Resolution 40 in the House of Representatives "expressing the sense of Congress that the United States should not engage in the construction of a NAFTA Superhighway System or enter into a North

American Union with Mexico and Canada." This resolution, as of September 2007, had 32 co-sponsors.

On July 24, 2007, the House of Representatives cast an historic first vote to restrict funding for the Security and Prosperity Partnership. The vote was 362 to 63 in favor of the resolution.

In addition, eighteen state legislatures are considering adopting anti-NAU resolutions. As of October 2007, three states have passed resolutions in both houses (Montana, Idaho, and Oklahoma). Fourteen other states have either introduced resolutions or one house of the legislature has passed similar resolutions.

The NAU will have no borders. All the current debate about immigration, the various proposed Federal legislative initiatives, and construction of a wall between the U.S. and Mexico has been deception and pacification by the Bush Administration and the bi-partisan globalists. The arrest and conviction of two U.S. Border Patrol Agents has George Bush's fingerprints on a scheme to prove to Mexico that the NAU would be a reality. They're simply buying time and diverting attention to their ultimate goal of no borders. The plan is so bold it is unbelievable. Take it from Jerome Corsi and the Oracle at Phoenix, it is *real*—and it is happening NOW. Join the groundswell.

Leadership

Lee Iacocca's latest book "Where Have All The Leaders Gone"[68] was published in 2007. Writing in the "straight-talk" manner that made him an icon in the auto business and corporate America, Lee says we're "in a hell of a mess."

"So here's where we stand. We're immersed in a bloody war with no plan for winning and no plan for leaving. We're running the biggest deficit in the history of the country. We're losing the manufacturing edge to Asia, while our once great companies are getting slaughtered by health care costs. Gas prices are sky-rocketing, and nobody in power has a coherent energy policy. Our schools are in trouble. Our borders are like

*sieves. The middle class is being squeezed every which way. These are
times that cry out for leadership.*

*But when you look around, you've got to ask: 'Where have all the
leaders gone?'...Where are the people of character, courage, conviction,
competence and common sense?'*

That, in "straight talk," just about says it all. Lee asks: "Am I the
only guy in this country who's fed up with what's happening? Where is the
outrage?"

Lee Iacocca and this author are on the same page and are deeply
concerned about the plight of America's middle class. Lee's mission is to
light a fire under Americans to stand up and be counted. He says, "You
can't call yourself a patriot if you're not outraged." *Greed* is not only
intended to educate but also to motivate you to action. The bottom line?
Problems don't get solved in Washington because our government is
broken, and no one has the leadership to fix it. The Oracle at Phoenix will
tell you why.

Lee almost entered politics in 1991 when Senator John Heinz was
killed in a plane crash. Governor Casey of Pennsylvania wanted to appoint
Lee to complete Heinz' term in the Senate to serve as a stepping stone to
the Presidency. The Democrats sent a "brash" young man by the name of
James Carville to meet with Lee and explain to him how the system
worked. Carville was "blunt and fast talking" and told Lee what his
position was to be on key issues. He didn't even elicit Lee's own views.
Lee advised Mr. Carville to take his position paper and 'shove it.'

This experience cuts directly to the root cause of "where have all the
leaders gone?" and why our democratic system of government is broken.
Imagine, if you will, George W. Bush's early meetings with the Republican
"neo cons" brain trust in 1999. But first, a little background.

Neo-conservatism is a political philosophy generally considered to
originate with Lee Strauss (1899-1973) who taught political science at the
University of Chicago. Strauss, borrowing from Machiavelli's "The Prince"
and "The Discourses" (which I studied keenly in college) advocated a

Machiavellian approach to governance. To rule, effectively, Strauss (and Machiavelli) believed that:

- A leader must perpetually deceive those being ruled.

- Religion is a force that binds a society together and is therefore a tool to be used by the ruler to control the masses.

- Secularism in society is to be suppressed.

- A political system can only be stable if it is united against an external threat. If no real threat exists, one should be manufactured.

One of Strauss' students was Paul Wolfowitz, who became a strategist in George W. Bush's U.S. Defense Department and was considered to be the architect of the Iraq War. In 1997, a group of ultra-conservatives formed a group called The Project for a New American Century (PNAC). This group, heavily invested in the defense industry, advocated a massive buildup and upgrading of U.S. weapons systems, ostensibly to bring democracy to countries under totalitarian control. One key aspect of the PNAC's mission was to recognize the strategic importance of Israel in America's global hegemony. PNAC members who now hold or have held positions in the Bush Administration are: Dick Cheney, Donald Rumsfeld, Paul Wolfowitz, Richard Perle, Eliot Abrams, Lewis Libby, and John Bolton, among others. William Kristol, a writer for the conservative magazine "Weekly Standard," is Chairman of PNAC. Perle, who was Chairman of Bush's Defense Policy Board, was referred to inside the Beltway as "The Prince of Darkness." Scary?

The purpose of this discourse should be apparent and disturbing. The PNAC strategy to effect a "regime change" in Iraq was developed <u>prior</u> to Al Qaida's attack on 9-11. The actual event provided an external threat to unify the country and the opportunity to secure the real objective—Iraq's oil, America's hegemony in the Middle East, and security for Israel.

George Bush's principal mission of governance was laid out for him, possibly as a pre-condition to gain financial support from the neo-cons. I suspect that included not only the regime change in Iraq but also pro-active support for the North American Union. There is no leadership in the White House. The President's first obligation was to the PNAC and those interests they represented, and not to the people he was elected to serve. Think Halliburton and Cheney. You're probably thinking that Bush, as a puppet for the PNAC, has a symbiotic relationship that was exclusive to the Republicans. Not so. The Clintons had their agenda also. Bill Clinton served his globalist masters well, despite all the baggage he carried to and from the oval office. Be most assured that Hillary, with the same support team intact, will have a similar agenda. Other than the NAU, the only question is: what is it? Just as in the case of the PNAC, we really didn't know before the election what the real agenda was.

Americans have begun to revolt and rail against a system that is not equal to the task of serving the critical needs of its citizens. We are a nation in deep trouble. Lee Iacocca's suggestion is to "throw all the bums out." Yes, we desperately need a third party—an independent third party beholden to no one but the people. Can and will it happen? Yes. Can it succeed? Therein lies the problem.

Ross Perot was the last serious independent candidate for President in 1992. Six months prior to the November election some polls rated the three candidates, Perot, Clinton and Bush (Sr.), almost dead even. In fact, for two months, Perot led the polls. A real threat to the two-party system that above all did not want the Presidency to pass to an "outsider." Suddenly, Perot announced that he was no longer a candidate—and his grass root supporters were devastated. Just as unexpectedly, Perot re-entered the race just prior to the election and managed to garner 18.9% of the popular vote. The question that may never be answered is: why did Perot withdraw at such a critical time ... which killed his momentum and led to his loss? Here is the Oracle at Phoenix's view outside the box.

Perot, a wealthy Texas businessman, was truly an outsider to the "establishment" and was not beholden to special interests. His principal rallying cry was against "the great sucking" sound that the North American Free Trade Agreement (NAFTA) represented. It would send American manufacturing jobs to Mexico and Latin America. This agreement that was so critical to the establishment of a framework for globalism, and what was to ultimately become the North American Union, could not be derailed ... and Perot, if elected, could cause its demise. Both Clinton and Bush and their parties strongly supported the "free trade" agreement. Perot had to be "neutralized." And he was.

Conclusion? There will never be a viable third party candidate in this country unless:

1. That person bows to the will of the Council on Foreign Relations (CFR) and other special interests, or

2. The American people unite and revolt in such numbers that they can over-ride the powers behind the throne that controls this country.

It's up to each and every one of us to reform the system and re-institute the Republic that we have lost.

A prime example of our broken system is reflected in the recently passed spending bill by Congress which has "unprecedented waste and corruption"[69] according to John Shadegg, who is the Author's Congressman for District 3 in Arizona.

The 3,417-page bill included 9,170 member-controlled projects (earmarks) combined with 2,161 passed earlier, totaling $20 billion. You'll recall that the 2006 Congress promised to be "the most ethical, honest and open Congress in history." In perhaps the most arrogant display of chutzpah, Congress resorted to the payoff system rewarding contributors, former staffers, and family members. Shadegg says that the approval "displays total disregard for both the legislative process and the Constitution." A dangerous precedent has been established, further demonstrating that the end game is near for the "late, great USA."

Freedom

You'll recall my earlier reference to George Orwell's "1984," Big Brother and one of the signs that was everywhere in Oceania, FREEDOM IS SLAVERY. What possibly could this contradiction in terms mean? And what place does this portent have in *Greed*?

The Outer Loop 101, a six-lane freeway, provides access to the Phoenix Metro area and at one point dissects the City of Scottsdale. Some motorists liken it to the autobahn in Germany. Excessive speed and a rash of fatal accidents prompted Scottsdale to introduce photo radar (aka Robo-Cop) perched above the freeway to discourage the speeders and reduce accidents. The response from the public was pronounced and predictable.

Many of the letters to the "Scottsdale Progress," the local newspaper, strongly criticized the City, stating that "Big Brother" was being employed to control their lives. I suspect few, if any, of the writers had ever read Orwell's novel, but they should. Implicit in many of the letters was the statement that this is no longer a free country and that driving over the speed limit was their business. And the rant went on for months, but there was little deterrence. You've probably experienced the same in your community.

One young lady received *twenty-two tickets* in a relatively short period of time for speeds of 90 to 100 mph. Her excuse? "I was late for work," Every day, we assume. A Ferrari was clocked at 150 mph! At that speed, as Bobby Unser once told me, you can't even sneeze because your eyes close for a second. The kamikaze Ferrari driver vowed to challenge the constitutionality of photo radar and asked the public to join him in his effort to curtail government intervention into our lives..

So, what is the message here?

**The Abuse of Freedom will
result in the Loss of Freedom**

and Ultimately

Freedom Is Slavery

There is a broader ramification to this micro view. In abusing this freedom of privilege and exhibiting a disrespect for law enforcement and the Rule of Law in all our endeavors, a limited number of Americans have given government the "authority" to restrict our freedom that will ultimately return our nation to the bonds of slavery. Look for this trend to manifest itself more prominently in the future. As Orwell saw in 1948, our TV will serve two masters.

The Crusade

Shortly after President Bush ordered the "shock & awe" bombing campaign against Iraq, I was delivering a talk on the economy to a political action group in Phoenix. During the Q&A period following my address, one of the attendees asked me:

"What is the long-term fallout from our war with Iraq?"

Without the luxury of time to contemplate my response, I said:

"President Bush has launched the third crusade. He has started a religious war that could last for a lifetime."

Not aware of it at the time, I was both prophetic and at the same time somewhat inaccurate.

The Crusades were a series of military campaigns during the Middle Ages initiated by Christians in Europe to free Jerusalem from the control of the Muslims. The first Crusade began in the year 1096 and lasted three years. There were a total of eight military excursions to the Middle East, the last occurring in the year 1210. I was in error. The Bush "Crusade" would be the ninth.

Obviously, the attack in Iraq was not a crusade to drive Muslims out of Jerusalem, but a point can legitimately be made that there are strong religious overtones to the conflict. Most Americans would not view it as such, but we should hear how the Muslims—and specifically Osama bin Laden—regard the war in which we find ourselves embroiled.

In Osama's own words stated on October 6, 2002:[70]

"If you Americans refuse to listen to our advice and the goodness, guidance, and righteousness that we call them to, then be aware that you will lose this Crusade that Bush began, just like the previous Crusades in which you were humiliated at the hands of the mujahidin, fleeing to your home in great silence and disgrace," p. 172.

Greed   H. L. Quist   Page 162

Little did I know at the time that my reference to Crusades is an accepted Muslim point of view.

As indicated in Chapter Nine under LEADERSHIP, in Osama the Neo-Cons had found their "external threat." The questions we all face are: How long will this threat continue and how entrenched is the Muslim resolve? Is the U.S. now entangled in a perpetual war just as the 2000-year conflict between the Muslims and the Jews?

Here are some insights in the thinking from the Al Qaida leader:

"You are a nation that permits usury, which has been forbidden by all the religions. Yet you build your economy and investments on usury ... the Jews have taken control of your economy, through which they have then taken control of your media and now control all aspects of your life making you their servants ... precisely what Benjamin Franklin warned you against." Ibid, p. 167.

"Your law is the law of the rich and wealthy, who hold sway in their political parties, and fund their election campaigns with their gifts." p. 168

And lastly:

"Do not interfere in our politics and method of education. Leave us alone, or else expect us in New York and Washington." p. 171.

As General George S. Patton, an avid war historian, once said, "Know everything about your enemy." It is clear from these messages that Osama's number one target is the U.S. economy and our free society. How vulnerable are we? Is there such a device as a nuclear suitcase bomb?

As to our vulnerability, the intent is clear and unambiguous. According to Senator Jon Kyl (R. Az) who previously served as Chairman of the U.S. Subcommittee on Terrorism, Technology and Homeland Security, numerous efforts by various terrorist groups over the last four or five years to create chaos have been successfully prevented by the Department of Homeland Security and other agencies. In an extensive AP article [71] "Suitcase Nukes Mostly Made in Hollywood" by Katherine Shader, a suitcase bomb was the focus of an entire season on the TV show "24." Experts say that a bomb of this type "... would be highly complex to produce, require significant upkeep (a nuclear core decomposes quickly), and cost a small fortune." Highly unlikely, but not impossible, that one could be detonated in the U.S.

In late November 2007 Slovak Police in Bratislava, Slovakia arrested three men accused of trying to sell for $1 million contraband uranium that was highly dangerous and could have been used in a radiological 'dirty bomb' or other terrorist weapon. Such a device could make Wall Street uninhabitable for years—an event that would have a horrendous impact on our economy. Much more likely.

The Neo-Cons are apparently planning a long-term occupation of Iraq. The Bushies are spending billions on a new embassy in Bagdad that resembles an impregnable fort rather than a diplomatic residence. U.S. taxpayers will soon have contributed *one trillion dollars* to this misguided mission with no prospect of withdrawal without chaos. The U.S. backed the Al Qaida to defeat the Russians in Afghanistan, which led to the financial collapse of the Soviet Union. The shoe is now on the other foot. Russia and other anti-U.S. protagonists now have the muscle and the money to bleed us to death in Iraq and the Middle East. (See "Charlie Wilson's War".) One of our nation's most critical geopolitical and financial decisions will have to be made by the next administration. A win/win option is no longer available.

A Neologism for a New World

The American Heritage Dictionary defines the above as "A newly coined word, phrase or expression ..." *Greed* has been a work of tediously compiling, organizing, and crafting together reams of data into a mosaic to educate the reader. The following neologism is this writer's attempt to create a symbolic representation that captures the essence of the political and economic dilemma with which all of us are now confronted.

Communism, in a theoretical sense, is a social and economic system characterized by the absence of social classes and a common (communal) ownership of property as well as production and distribution of all goods and services. A ruling elite exercises absolute control over all aspects of the society and the economy. For purposes here we will use China and Russia as examples of Communist governments.

The People's Republic of China (PRC) is controlled by the Communist Party of China (CPC), and currently Hu Jintao is General Secretary of the CPC and Chairman of the PRC elected solely by his party's peers. The Chinese began a program of "social modernization" in 1978 which introduced elements of free market capitalism to the nation, which has catapulted the country to its prominent role in the global economy in less than 30 years.

Russia's departure from a Marxist centrally managed economy occurred abruptly in 1992 when the government collapsed. After a period of social, political, and economic chaos, Vladamir Putin became President of Russia in 2000. Despite his well-chronicled battles with Russia's new breed of capitalists (the oligarches), the economy has flourished. Unable to serve more than two terms, Putin will assume the position of Prime Minister in 2008 and will continue to exercised political control of the country. In short, both China and Russia have adopted elements of free market capitalism while retaining strict political control.

In contrast, the U.S. has demonstrated and proclaimed for more than two centuries that its economic model has produced unrivaled success, because it embodied both free market capitalism and an open democratic society.

The great irony in this collectivist shift is while the two communist giants have borrowed from our capitalist economic model and at the same time retained centralized control, the U.S. has borrowed a page from the

Red's play book! Incrementally, the U.S. is moving away from a democratic form of government and consolidating power in the hands of a ruling elite.

Nonsense, you say? The U.S. is a government "of the people, by the people, and for the people" you say?

Is it:

- When a President and his administration adhering to a Machiavellian approach to governance create an "external threat" to our country and commit hundreds of thousands of serviceman and women and a trillion dollars in order to consolidate their political power and profit a military industrial complex that drains the human and financial resources of the country;

- When the people's elected representatives brazenly continue the corrupt practice of earmarks with no fear of rebuke from their constituents;

- When the penultimate goal of each political party is to subvert the Constitution of the United States of America which they have sworn to defend;

- When the executive branch of our government can induce the judicial branch to prosecute U.S. government employees whose only crime was protecting the interests of their country in one of the most blatant miscarriages of justice in the history of the United States; and

- When our representatives spend more time, more effort, and more money getting elected than effecting the people's business;

Then, in the opinion of this author, our leaders are merging our capitalist economic model with the collectivism of communism. The neologism?

Copulativism

Chapter Ten
The Crack-up Boom

While discussing *Greed* with my focus group and others that I've interviewed for contributions to this book, the overriding question is (understandably): What direction do you see for the real estate market? Or the stock market? As Yogi Berra was once reported to have said, "Making predictions is difficult because it's about the future."

I'm a firm believer that we all need to step back after we've analyzed all the data and try to grasp the macro-economic picture before we try to determine how our microcosm is impacted—whether it be real estate, the stock market, the retail market, or any other arena that pertains to your business and interest. That's what I'm best equipped to do—give you the "big picture." It will also be a view from "outside the box." Chances are you'll be surprised ... but more importantly, prepare yourself for an unexpected and unique opportunity.

As the year 2007 comes to an end, a consensus is emerging on the economy. A poll of 52 economists in the U.S. revealed that 38% of them forecasted that the nation would enter a recession in 2008. Alan Greenspan upped his prediction of a recession to 50% for the New Year. Numerous real estate experts are indicating that the supply/demand balance in the residential market won't return to normal until 2009 at the earliest. And some pundits indicate that the "Freeze the Teaser" program that curtails any interest increases in ARMs for five years will protract and delay the residential recovery period rather than reduce it. As you will recall from Chapter One, it took a little better than three years for the economy and the real estate market to recover from the 1990 bust, so precedent has been established.

Conventional wisdom indicates that the above general scenario of an economic slowdown will have a duration of three years. There is, however, a totally different dynamic that could assert itself which has little precedent in the U.S. This phenomenon was described by Ludwig Von Mises as a "Crack-up-Boom." As this is written (December 2007), we're entering a recession in the economy or, in terms previously stated in **Greed,** a "Bust." As you've learned, there is normally a period of time after a bust before the economy recovers. A time when the excesses in the market that caused the boom are dissolved and "absorbed into the system." What, then, would cause a sudden boom to occur, thereby reducing or eliminating the time for the economy to slowly recover from the recession? Specifically, what would cause a sudden rise in real property values in a matter of months rather than years? And what would cause the U.S. equity markets to boom to new highs at levels no one on Wall Street (even Larry Kudlow and Jim Cramer) would ever expect? In this scenario, Goldilocks becomes one hot tomato!

A "Crack-up-Boom," according to Von Mises, [72] occurs when citizens begin to question the value of their currency and are motivated to exchange it for an asset that they have more faith in that will hold the value. He goes on to say:

"The boom can last only as long as the credit expansion progresses at an ever-accelerated pace. The boom comes to an end as soon as additional quantities of fiduciary media are no longer thrown upon the loan market. But it could not last forever even if inflation and credit expansion were to go on endlessly. It would then encounter the barriers which prevent the boundless expansion of circulation credit. It would lead to the crack-up boom and the breakdown of the whole monetary system.

The credit expansion boom is built on the sands of banknotes and deposits. It must collapse. If the credit expansion is not stopped in time, the boom turns into the crack-up boom; the flight into real values begins, and the whole monetary system founders. Continuous inflation (credit expansion) must finally end in the crack-up boom and the complete breakdown of the currency system.

The Fed, the U.S. Treasury, and the insatiable desire amongst our corporate and political leaders to globalize the world's economy have created near perfect conditions to create a "Crack-up-Boom." What is different this time is that virtually all the world's central banks are advocates of a fiat (paper) money and the creation of excessive easy credit, and this makes the potential event world-wide rather than confined to one country.

There is one assumption that makes the probability of a boom of this nature a distinct possibility. The Merchants of Debt (MOD) and the politicians will do anything to prevent a global contraction and deflation—the dreaded "Double D"—Depression and Default. As a result, we will see the other extreme scenario—inflation, or even hyperinflation—and ultimately a "Crack-up Boom."

The overriding issue today in the U.S. economy is that real estate values are declining, and in the case of the CDOs, the debt on the homes is much greater than the asset. There is no equity ... and that situation is spreading to Alt-A and Prime loans. Debt is a constant. It's fixed. It's the value of the collateral that can change. Inflation will increase the value of the home and will restore equity. A little inflation, therefore, is good. Hyperinflation will end badly. Given the tenuousness of the situation today, a little inflation would bail out many banks and homeowners, but controlling inflation once the citizens realize what is happening to the value of their money is challenging at best. It's like getting *a little* pregnant ... it has not yet been done.

There is anecdotal evidence everywhere to support Von Mises' theory. Rather than tightening credit, U.S. banks are layering new credit on past non-performing debt. At a time when credit card default rates are rising dramatically, as noted earlier, the issuers of plastic mailed out 1.29 billion card offers to U.S. households during the last quarter—and 363 million went to "high-risk" families. Synovate, a market research firm, says that high-risk households continue to receive 6.5 credit card offers per month![73] Now we know why consumer spending continued unabated during the 2007

Christmas season. It's this lack of discipline and continued availability of credit that fuels an inflationary boom.

"Vulture Funds," so named because they're feeding on carcasses in the real estate market, are beginning to flap their wings, devouring distressed properties. One big name player is Sam Zell, who earned the nickname "Grave Dancer" in the 70s for buying real estate on the cheap when the market was in the toilet after the oil embargo. Zell sold his real estate firm at the top of the market in 2006 and now is looking for depressed commercial properties that he can "monetize" through a publicly held company or Real Estate Investment Trust (REIT). His plan is to sell shares to global investors who regard U.S. real assets as cheap due to the declining dollar. His timing could be perfect.

As cited earlier, the oil exporters, flush with devaluing U.S. dollars, are buying U.S. assets on the prospect that there will be a renaissance or resurgence in our nation's asset value, short term and long term. Eurozone countries faced with the appreciation of the euro versus the U.S. dollar are building or restoring manufacturing plants in the U.S. in order to be globally competitive. The twist here in manufacturing is, indeed, a little ironic. The U.S. loses manufacturing jobs to China. The decline in the U.S. dollar makes imports from China more expensive so China builds plants in the US. The cheap dollar also makes European exports considerably more costly, so the Brits and the Germans set up manufacturing plants in the U.S. to sell to Americans and export back to Europe. What it all means is an unexpected boost to the economy from an unanticipated source which helps to kindle the boom.

Perhaps the greatest influence on and the greatest contributor to the "Crack-up Boom" is the coming global energy crisis. The world is approaching the end of the age of oil. Virtually all of the major oil fields in Prudhoe Bay, Mexico, North Sea, Saudi Arabia, and others have already or will soon reach peak production. Illustrated on a Bell Curve, an oil field's production will gradually ramp up until it reaches its peak ... then the curve drops sharply as the field is depleted. Production in the U.S. reached its peak in 1970. IHS Energy Inc.[74] estimates that worldwide today, only one barrel of oil is being discovered for every six extracted, while consumption increases unabatedly. Alternative sources will not be implemented in time to avoid a crisis. Unless there is a global recession or depression, the price of oil will rise dramatically in the next ten years. Think $200 per barrel and $100 to fill your tank.

Amongst the "apologists" that are called upon to dispute or ameliorate all economic data on CNBC and other media outlets are those who claim that higher oil and gasoline prices no longer have an effect on the inflation that persisted in the late 1970s. The Bureau of Labor Statistics (BOLS) excludes food and energy from the "core" inflation numbers, which adds to the illusion that higher energy costs are not detrimental to the economy.

This contention is absolute nonsense. Higher prices are currently impacting virtually everything we consume (have you shopped for food lately?), and manufacturers have to pass on their increased costs to the end user or absorb the loss. In a "Crack-up Boom" expect prices to increase for all goods and services and capital goods—slowing at first in 2008, then ratcheting up rapidly in 2009 and beyond. Then, suddenly, the economy will "crack up," and all prices will decline in a classic deflationary contraction.

Amongst all the alternative energy sources, nuclear is the most viable and cheapest source to meet the demand for electricity. Five years ago when the world was oblivious (but your author saw the future) to the explosive demand for electricity, uranium ore (the fuel stock for nuclear power plants) was a minuscule $7/lb. When the electricity began to shut off in China and the Chinese saw the light, uranium ore rose to a price of $140/lb. There has since been a correction back to a more realistic level of $95/lb., but China will build 20 or more nuclear plants over the next ten years. The U.S. will also see its first new plants to be permitted soon, the first in thirty years. But it's the next five to ten years when the fit will hit the shan.

As indicated earlier, inflation is a monetary phenomenon. The Greenspan Plan in 2001 created more debt that "incentivised" homeowners and speculators to dig themselves a deeper hole to get the banks out of the one *they* were already in. For five years the scheme worked as real property values ballooned and exceeded the debt. But now the situation has reversed, and debt (in many cases) exceeds the value of the collateral. Worse yet, the mortgage mess has created a world-wide liquidity crunch. What do the bankers do now? (You should know the answer by now.)

Create more debt, of course!

On December 12, 2007, the Fed announced that it would extend up to $40 billion in loans via an auction to banks to ease the banks' concerns about their own ability to borrow. The European Central Bank as well as the British, Swiss, and Canadian Central Banks also agreed to "prime" their nation's banks with additional cash to loan to customers. In December the European Central Bank lent an unprecedented $501 billion (USD) to its member banks to provide funds to lend. In moving to cure the anxiety over insolvency, the central banks expose themselves to debasing their currencies which, of course, is what makes inflation a monetary phenomenon. This move was in addition to billions previously injected into the U.S. banks in the past three months. Historically, any time the central banks have created this much liquidity, a boom soon follows.

I have told past clients for years that in the early stages of an inflation cycle be fully invested in all asset classes (like January 2003). Conversely, in the late stages, liquidate all assets prior to the inevitable bursting of the inflationary bubble. An historical perspective will be helpful.

Hyperinflation has been described as a condition where the prices of goods and services increase at an annualized rate of 25% or more. The only time that happened in the U.S. was in the Confederate States of America during the Civil War (1861-1865). The most dramatic and ruinous case of hyperinflation occurred in Germany after WWI. During the War the mark was almost at parity with the U.S. dollar. By 1923 the exchange rate was

1,000,000 marks to one U.S. dollar. My parents could recall the stories that it took a wheelbarrow of marks to buy a loaf of bread. Those who borrowed money saw their debt extinguished. Those who lent marks or lived on fixed incomes saw their loan receivable or their retirement income go to zero. Maybe those Americans who are up to their eyeballs in debt actually know what they're doing ... they'll never pay it back!

Any student of the global economy will recall the devastating hyperinflation in Latin America in the 1980s. Argentina is a very recent example how the "Crack-up Boom" manifested itself.

Twenty years of deficit spending and bad fiscal management resulted in 200% per month hyperinflation in Argentina by 1990. Carlos Menem was elected President to quell the hyperinflation. He adopted a *laissez-faire* policy and attracted much-needed foreign capital to the country. He tied the Argentina peso to the U.S. dollar and for a short period of time brought stability and prosperity to his country. Unfortunately, the strong peso tied to a strong dollar worked against him, and the country elapsed into a recession in 1995. Suddenly and unexpectedly, however, there was a "Crack-up Boom" lasting from 1996 to 1998. Some Argentines, now accustomed to repeated devaluation of their fiat pesos, exchanged their currency for dollars ... but the economy collapsed again in 1999. Argentina, which was once the fourth largest economy in the world, defaulted on its sovereign debt as the country suffered from a severe recession.

Argentines could survive the hyperinflation boom by going to the nearest Citigroup Bank and convert their pesos to U.S. dollars—but that was then. Now and in the future in a globalized economy where the former almighty U.S. dollar will no longer the world's reserve currency, where will people go to protect their buying power in a "Crack-up Boom?"

Here's the unexpected surprise:

1. The Stock Market

At present the U.S. stock market is over-bought and over-valued. There could be a near-term nasty correction of 10% to 30% in early

2008, but that could be the trigger point for an explosive rally that will carry the indices well beyond their all-time highs. Think 20,000 on the Dow Jones Industrial Average. The highest returns should be in emerging markets. The end of the "Crack-up Boom" will signal the beginning of a severe bear market. When? It will depend on the velocity of the boom. A rapid inflationary cycle would result in a short boom of one to two years. A slow rise could extend the boom for three years or more.

2.   Real Estate (Residential)

Investors and home buyers who bought in the trough of the market in 2007 and 2008 could realize excellent gains within several years. Vulture funds, investors, and foreign buyers will absorb supply. Home prices in the major markets like Phoenix should exceed the highest values at the top of the 2006 market within two years and reach a level never envisioned attainable until the "Crack-up Boom" ends. Seniors who didn't cash out at the top of 2006 will have a second chance for $500,000 in tax-free gains.

3.   Precious Metals

Gold, which has risen in value from $255/oz. to over $800/oz. in the past five years could exceed $2,000/oz. at the height of the "Crack-up Boom." Adjusted for inflation, gold would have to reach $2,200/oz. to equal its previous high in 1980, which was an inflationary boom. Silver should follow in gold's footsteps. For the average investor, a gold mutual fund or an Exchange Traded Fund (ETF) would be the most viable method to insure against the loss of the currency's value in a "Crack-up Boom" (whether it be the U.S. dollar or Amero). When the "Crack-up" occurs, this asset class should be liquidated. When deflation comes, cash will be king in any currency.

4.   Commodities

All commodities, including energy, grains, meats, precious metals, etc. have reflected (and will continue to reflect) the monetary phenomenon known as inflation. There could be a correction in prices in early 2008 due to recession fears, which would represent a buying opportunity. The Commodity Research Bureau (CRB) tracks the price movements of 22 basic commodities. The CRB Index has risen from 394 to 475 in the past year and has been in a dramatic bullish uptrend for the past five years. The grains alone have risen from 271 to 429 in 2007, as wheat has reached an all-time high of $11/bushel from $4/bushel in the last five years. The best way for the average investor to participate in this market is by purchasing shares in an ETF. Another product (not considered a commodity) whose demand will exceed its supply is potable water. Investors can also participate in this market by purchasing shares of an ETF And don't forget uranium mining. It's the fuel of the future, and stocks are cheap.

For certain, there are a number of other alternatives in event there is a "Crack-up Boom," and those above are only a general suggestion. Any action taken by the reader should be discussed with their financial advisor. A boom will necessitate another book to prepare for the "crack-up."

America, and indeed the world, is in the midst of the greatest technological, social, economic, and political change in modern history. Incredible opportunities and cavernous pitfalls will present themselves. My hope is that *Greed* will open your eyes so that you can see the pitfalls and the opportunities and that you will profit from the good and avoid the bad.

End Notes

1. Sandra Ward, *Investing In a Shaky World*, Barron's, 9-18-06, p. 46.

2. Addison Wiggin, <u>The Demise of The Dollar, And Why it is Great For Your Investments</u>, published by John Wiley & Sons, Inc., Hoboken, NJ 2005, p. 14-16

3. Susan Pulliam and Serena Ng, *Partners in Credit Deals Face Big Write-Downs As Bond Insurer Teeters*, Wall Street Journal, January 18, 2008.

4. Arizona Republic, Corp. For Enterprise Development.

5. Rachel Beck, *Mortgage Spreads to Other Debt*, AP, Arizona Republic, November 7, 2007, p. D-1

6. Social Class in the US, Wikipedia, The Free Encyclopedia.

7. James Bovard, *Nothing Down,* Barron's 8-23-04, p. 31

8. Jonathan R. Laing, Barron's 6-20-05, p. 24-26, *The Bubble's New Home*, an interview with Robert Shiller

9. Nang Nguyen, Orange Co. Register, 5-24-05 "Greenspan Calls Housing Price Growth' Unsustainable."

10. Ruth Simon, Wall Street Journal, 7-26-05 "Mortgage Lenders Loosen Standards," p. D 1-2.

11. Jonathan R. Laing, *Garbage In, Carnage Out*, Barron's, 7-09-07, p. 21-22.

12. Jonathan Laing, *Subprime's Ultimate Time Bomb*, Barron's, 08-06-07, p. 16.

13. Aaron Lucchetti and Serena Ng, Wall Street Journal, *How Ratings Firms Calls Fueled SubPrime Mess*, 8-15-07, p. A 1, 10.

14. Carrick Mollenkamp and Ian McDonald, *Behind Sumprime Woes, A Cascade of Bad Debts*, Wall Street Journal, October 17, 2007, p. A-1, 16.

15. Peter A. McKay & Justin Lenhart, *Boom in Buy Backs Help Lift Stocks to Record Highs*, Wall Street Journal, 7-18-07, p. D-1

16. Global Business Briefs, Wall Street Journal, October 31, 2007, p. .

17. Steven Rattner, *The Coming Credit Meltdown*, Wall Street Journal, 8-18-07.

18. Gregory Zuckerman & Serena Ng, Boom Aside, Not All LBO's Look So Hot, 8-08-07, p. C-1

19. George Anders, KKR, *Blackstone IPO's Put Their Style at Risk*, Wall Street Journal, 7-17-07, p. A-2.

20. Tennile Tracy, *Its The Fees, Not The Profits*, Wall Street Journal, 9-13-07, p. C-1

21. David Rocker, *Wall Street Borrows, Main Street Pays*, Barron's, 9-17-07, p. 59.

22. Joe Bel Bruno, *Goldman Sachs Profits Rise Amid Mortgage Turbulence*, AP, 9-21-07.

23. Alan Greenspan, *The Age of Turbulence, Adventures in a New World*, The Penguin Press, New York, 2007.

24. Brian Doherty, *Rand & The Right*, Wall St. Journal, 10-10-07, opinion.

25. Bill Laggner & George Karahalios, Strategic Investment, 10/2007, *Collateral Damage*, p. 2-5

26. Carrick Mollenkamp, Deborah Selowan & Robin Sidel, *U.S. Plays Role in Banks' Talks on Rescue Fund*, Wall Street Journal, 10-15-07, p. A-16.

27. Opinion, *House of Paulson*, Wall Street Journal, 10-16-07, p. A-20

28. Thomas G. Donlan, *No More Toxic Cleanups*, Barrron's, 10-22-07,

29. E. S. Browning, *Fed Treads Moral Hazard*, Wall Street Journal, 08-13-07, P. A-1.

30. Rick Brooks, Constance Mitchell Ford, *The United States of Subprime*, Wall Street Journal, 10-11-07, p. A-1, 16.

31. Catherine Reagor, *Foreclosure Filings in Valley Soar 566% in '07*, Arizona Republic, November 10, 2007.

32. *Focus: Foreclosures Increase Suburban Crime*, AP, Arizona Republic, November 15, 2007, p. D-5.

33. Jacqueline Doherty, *Homebuilders' Woes Are Far From Over*,

Barron's, October 1, 2007, p. 20.

34.   Jeannine Aversa, *Greenspan Didn't See Danger of Subprimes*, Arizona Republic, 09-14-07, p. D-1.

35.   Gerald P. O'Driscoll, Jr., Opinion, *Our Subprime Fed*, Wall Street Journal, 08-10-07, P. A-11.

36.   Alan Abelson, *Go Figure*, Barron's, 10-08-07, p. 5.

37.   Alan Abelson, Up & Down Wall St., *On Borrowed Time*, Barrons, 08/20/07, p. 27-8.

38.   Alan Abelson, *Call To ARMS*, Barron's 06-26-07, Up & Down Wall Street, P., 7-8

39.   Gene Epstein, *Growth Will Survive Fed's Best Efforts*, Barron's, 03-26-07, Economic Beat, p. 53.

40.   Gene Epstein, *The Case for A Half-Point Fed-Funds Cut*, Barron's, 09-17-07, Economic Beat, p. 55.

41.   Damien Paletta, *Fed Feels Pressure to Protect Consumers*, Wall Street Journal, 07-17-07, Politics & Economics, p. A-8.

42.   Stuart M. Saft, *The Anit-Mortgage Act*, Wall Street Journal, November 10, 2007.

43.   Peggy Noonan, *Now He Tells Us*, Wall Street Journal, 09-22-07 "Declarations".

44.   Randall Smith & Serena Ng, *Metro PCS Sues Merrill Over Risky Investments*, Wall Street Journal, 10-19-07.

45.   Opinion, *Ex-Prince of the City*, Wall Street Journal, November 6, 2007, p. A-18.

46.   Henry Kaufman, *Our Risky Financial Markets*, Wall Street Journal, 08-15-07.

47.   Jeannine Aversa, *Fed Targets Abuses in Home Loans*, AP, Arizona Republic, December 16, 2007, p. A-9

48.   Jonathan R. Laing, *Getting Ready for the Roof to Fall*, Barron's, 10-01-07, p. 26-27.

49.   J. S. Elphinstone (AP), *Mortgage Bailout Stirs Controversy*, The Arizona Republic, p. D-5.

50. John Bercase, *The Subprime FHA*, Wall Street Journal, 10-15-07, p. A-23.

51. Randall W. Forsyth, Current Yield, *Defining Delinquency Down*, Barron's, December 3, 2007, P. M-14.

52. Aaron Lucchetti, *A New Mortgage "Cop"*, Wall Street Journal, 10-08-07, p. C-1

53. *U.S. Mortgage Crisis Rivals S&L Meltdown*, Wall Street Journal, December 10, 2007, p. A-1 & 16.

54. Thomas G. Donlan, *Giving Credit Where Due,"* Barron's, August 20, 2007, p. 39.

55. Wikipedia, The Internet Free Encyclopedia.

56. Lawrence J. Kotlikoff and Scott Burns, <u>The Coming Generational Storm: What You Need to Know About America's Economic Future</u>.

57. H. L. Quist, *The Future Isn't What It Used To Be*, July, 2005.

58. Making Piece, December 1, 2007.

59. James P. Owen and David R. Stoecklin, <u>Cowboy Ethics: What Wall Street Can Learn from the Code of the West</u>, Stoecklin Publishing Co., Ketchum, Idaho, 2004.

60. Wikipedia, The Internet Free Encyclopedia.

61. Ibid, p. 463

62. Ibid, p. 483

63. Ibid, p. 478

64. Wikipedia, The Internet Free Encyclopedia.

65. Jerome R. Corsi, *"The Late Great USA: The Coming Merger with Mexico and Canada"*, WND Books, Los Angeles, CA, 2007.

66. Time   Article   from   1998, http://www.time.com/time/time100/builder/profile/walton.html

67. Larry Greenly, *Signs of Hope*, The New American, October 15, 2007, p. 43.

68. Lee Iacocca with Catherine Whitney, <u>Where Have All The Leaders Gone</u>, Scribner , 1230 Avenue of the Americas, New York, NY, 10020. 2007

69.   John Shadegg, *Congress Rips Off Tax Payers Again*, Arizona Republic, December 5, 2007, p. B-5.

70. Messages to the World, The Statements of Osama Bin Laden, Edited and Introduced by Bruce Lawrence, Translated by James Howarth, Verso Publishing Co., New York.

71. "Suitcase Nudes Mostly Made in Hollywood" by Katherine Shader, Arizona Republic, November 11, 2007. P. A-24.

72. Ludwig Von Mises Institute Website

73.   Russ Wiles, "Spotlight Lingers on Credit Ills", Arizona Republic, December 9, 2007, p. D-5

74.   Carolyn L. Baker, "US History Uncensored", Peak Oil & Global Resource Wars, p. 184